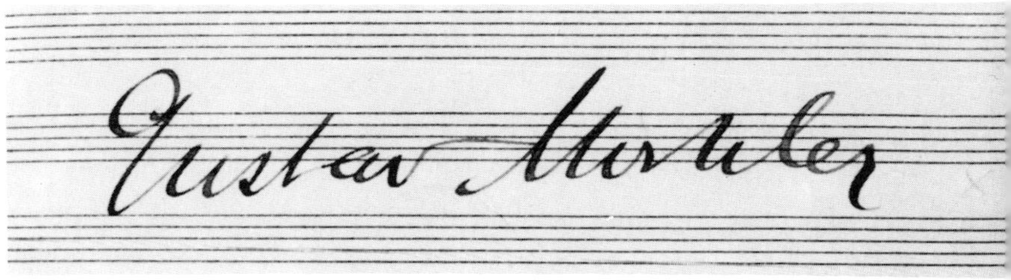
Gustav Mahler

GUSTAV MAHLER IN VIENNA

CONTRIBUTORS
PIERRE BOULEZ · FRIEDRICH C. HELLER
HENRY-LOUIS DE LA GRANGE · MARCEL PRAWY
WOLF ROSENBERG · GOTTFRIED SCHOLZ
HILDE SPIEL · SIGRID WIESMANN

EDITED BY
SIGRID WIESMANN

TRANSLATED BY
ANNE SHELLEY

DESIGNED BY
JAROSLAV KREJCI

RIZZOLI
INTERNATIONAL PUBLICATIONS
NEW YORK

"It is music that is full of human frailties, no doubt. But when all is said, there remains something extraordinarily touching about the man's work, something that makes one willing to put up with the weaknesses. Perhaps this is because his music is so very Mahler-like in every detail. All his nine symphonies are suffused with personality – he has his own way of saying and doing everything. The irascible scherzos, the heaven-storming calls in the brass, the special quality of his communings with nature, the gentle melancholy of a transitional passage, the gargantuan Ländler, the pages of an incredible loneliness – all these, combined with the above-mentioned histrionics, an inner warmth, and the will to evoke the largest forms and the grandest musical thoughts, add up to one of the most fascinating composer-personalities of modern times."

AARON COPLAND

Gustav Mahler in the loggia of the Vienna Opera, 1907. The armchair is the one Mahler also used at his desk.

Gustav Mahler

"Instead of speaking at great length, perhaps I would do better simply to say: 'It is my firm, unshakable belief that Gustav Mahler, the man and the artist, was one of the greatest.' For indeed there are only two ways in which one can convince others of an artist's ability: the first – and better – way, is to perform his work and the second, which I am obliged to make use of, is to communicate to others my belief in his work."

ARNOLD SCHÖNBERG

Gustav Mahler on the way to the Imperial Opera, 1904.

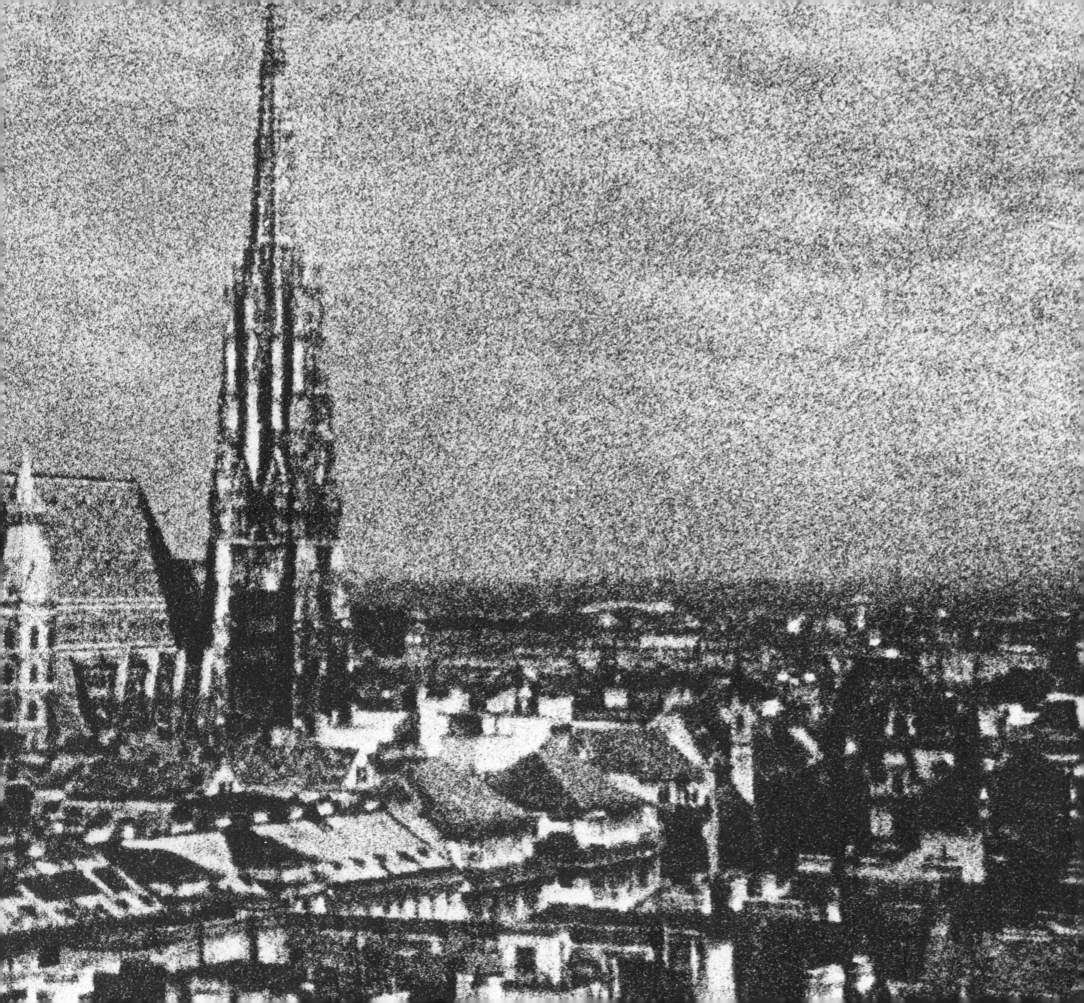

Pierre Boulez

GUSTAV MAHLER UP-TO-DATE?

How long it took until he stepped forth, not from the shadows but from purgatory! A long lasting purgatory that held him prisoner for a thousand reasons: too much of a conductor, not enough of a composer; and moreover a composer who could not disengage himself from being a conductor; too much dexterity and skill, too little mastery. And, what is more, he kept mixing it all up! Opera, of which he was a passionate conductor, hardly entered into his own work at all; whereas the noble symphonic domain was abused by heaps of the bad theatrical seed: sentimentality, vulgarity, disorder, each arrogant and repulsive, noisily and massively pushing its way into this well-guarded territory.

Meanwhile a group of enthusiastic admirers keeps watch during his posthumous exile, fanatics from two easily separable camps: the Progressives and the Conservatives; the latter boast of being the true defenders of his work, convinced that it had been betrayed by the former. And then the black mark of being a Jew, in a period of frantic nationalism. The memory of this outcast, who in his own country is condemned to silence, fades until his shadow is no longer recognizable. And then the myth in which Mahler and Bruckner unceasingly appear as Castor and Pollux of the Symphony. After Beethoven it is impossible to go beyond Nine; the symphonic

Left: The bust of Gustav Mahler by Auguste Rodin which he made in 1907; a replica of the cast is on display in the foyer of the Vienna Opera.

dynasty will be cursed by destiny should it dare to advance beyond that fateful number. (In the meantime, however, some less gifted composers have accomplished this heroic feat.) What could be salvaged from this catastrophe?

The memory of an extraordinary and difficult, pitiless and eccentric conductor. Some of his scores, the shortest, easiest, most readily approachable. For a long time this had to suffice. The traditional symphonic appetite was appeased with other, less complex, less demanding time-fillers. The sparse performances were unable to create a following, what they left behind was doubt, not only of the intrinsic value but of the sincerity of such a project. On the other hand the Moderns had passed him by, had consigned him to the dead stock of an outlived romanticism, lacking in contemporaneous interest and looked upon with a kind of pity. Everything in this *fin-de-siècle* music, the whole excessive profusion, went against the grain while economy became more and more the watchword. The reckless extension of time, the surplus of instruments, the supercharged feelings and gestures... form had to break down under such excesses! What can be the value of music whose relation of idea and form loses itself in the nether regions of expression? Here we touch on the end of a world which ruins its digestion through luxury, which drowns in superabundance; foolish arrogance is the worst and a sentimental apopletic fit the best that can happen to such a world. Begone, obese and degenerate romanticism!

Begone? If the works insist on survival there is no begone... You repudiate them? Even vehemently? But the works insist on remaining. Wonderful!

Now that the time of cleansing is past we see that it has left some true skeletons behind in its path. But after this long period of inattention the authentic emerges once more, forces us to consider anew and stubbornly questions our negligence.

Were we guilty, were we superficial? Can we offer justifications? By the manner in which this work was presented to us – guarded by certainly devout but fanatically greedy hands (hands without that generosity which paves the way of the future by the means of the past), monopolized by the faithful (at what point does loyalty become treason?) – this work was capable of imbuing us with a full measure of distrust. A distrust that even made us suspect that the composers of the Vienna school had succumbed to a sentimental, locally coloured attachment. At first glance, to be sure, the link was not obvious, the antinomies instead quite clear.

But after the Moderns had finished with ascesis, exuberance got hold of the consciousness – and the search of the past began, enriched by new modes of hearing, though the mind, alerted by recent experience, kept watch with painfully acquired vigilance.

Left: Gustav Mahler in 1907.

Probably tired of clear directions, one-dimensional meanings, the mind dreams of multiplicities, of a world where the categories are too complicated to be understood too easily.

Order? Why this constraining word?

All right! Let us forget about all these constraining concepts: order, definition of ideas, of style, clarity of structure. For the time being let us get rid of these paralyzing notions. But is it so simple? Certainly not! Especially if one is not willing to be coerced by external circumstances. How difficult it is, especially in the case of Mahler, to steer free of the legend which stubbornly mingles life and work, immediate life experience and artistic creation, melodrama and agony. Let us then give the enthusiastic exegesis its due and let us unstintingly face the dissimilar monuments he left behind.

First of all we are put off by a seeming dilemma: the borderline between sentimentality and irony, nostalgia and criticism which it is sometimes impossible to define. There is no real contradiction but the swing of a pendulum, a sudden change of the light which makes for revelations of certain musical ideas, which one first senses as being banal, unnecessary, but then indispensable, after they have traversed this difficult prism. The banality for which he was so often blamed in the beginning and which looked like a lack of creative imagination: does one still find it insufferable? Is it not the humus of a widespread mistake concerning the "popular"? *Prima facie* hearing often gets stuck on easy clichés, treacle – sweet but empty words, an entire fading and quickly disappearing landscape from a past that is remembered in vignettes. Some are delighted, some disgusted – and it makes it impossible for both to get beyond this first impression which is merely an antechamber...

Yes, this material indeed exists. Sometimes it may seem limited, excessively predictable; the source hardly changes from one work to the next. After quoting the march and all its military and funereal derivatives, the dances in three-quarter time (Ländler, waltzes or minuets), the whole regional repertory of folklore, we have just about drawn the circle around this "borrowed" and easily defined source of themes. From the first to the last work there is one obviously constant quality: these are clichés, inherited from "elevated" or "lowbrow" history.

At the opposite side of this reservoir of "banalities" is an array of huge theatrical gestures, heroic and sublime – music of the spheres and of infinity; a dimension of grandiosity of which the worst that can be said is that some of its intensity has faded. But why is it that these gestures, which are dead in other composers, still retain the power of their pathos? Could it be that these gestures, far from pretending to be

Gustav Mahler

Emil Orlik, the painter, was one of the few artists who portrayed Gustav Mahler as conductor. Left: An ink drawing. Right: Two head studies.

triumphal, cover an enormous measure of insecurity? How far away in the past lies the self-assured romanticism, so proud of its heroism! And how far away is the naïvité of the first approach to the sources of folklore. In Mahler's world no one can fail to hear his nostalgia; but, like it or not, it must share its territory with criticism, even sarcasm. Why sarcasm? Is that not the ultimate of an unmusical characteristic? Music, we know, likes undisguised meanings and is not happy in this double-faced play of irony and sincerity. One never can tell: what is now truth, what caricature? Orientation is not very difficult with a text, but what about "absolute" music?

Double-entendre, persiflage, can only really be understood with the background of a text based on accepted and well known conventions. For this game of "funny mirrors" all that is often necessary is simply to distort the conventions: exaggerated or misplaced emphasis, condensed or stretched-out tempo, unusual, prismatic, chopped-up instrumentation. The aggressive humour is not satisfied until everything is enveloped in unreal, ghostly colour, the original object penetrated by X-rays and appearing to us now as a jumble of black boughs and branches which shake us up and jolt us out of our familiar ways: a world of fleshless, rattling bones, realistically evoked by bizarre, nay grotesque, combinations of sound; a world born of a nightmare and ready any time to return to it; a world of shadows, a world without colour, a world of ashes, a world without matter. How avidly it is captured, how pitilessly illustrated – this world of spectres in which memory goes to pieces!

What is it that attracts us – is it merely the sentimental, bizarre or sarcastic reflexes of a dwindling world which a keenly perspicacious man knew how to catch? Is this sufficient to hold our attention and enthrall us? The reason for the fascination today surely lies in that hypnotic ability to project a vision that passionately embraces the end of an era; an era which inexorably had to wilt away so that another could rise in its place. This music describes the myth of the Phoenix almost too literally.

On the other side of this sunset spectacle that revolution takes place – surprisingly – with which he shatters the world of symphony. With what determination, even wildness, he attacks the hierarchy of these forms which had been modified before his time but were now congealed in a strict and decorative convention. Was it the stage which drove him towards this dramatic destruction of compelling and constricting forms? Just as Wagner overthrew the artificial code of opera in order to evoke in his music drama a vastly more demiurgic process, so too Mahler revolutionizes the symphony, devastates this all too cultivated terrain, infiltrates the Holy of Holies of logic with his hallucinations. Does not Beethoven rise up here as the true model, this barbarian who in his time abundantly sowed disorder and chaos? And

also as model for the extension, an extension beyond all "reason" of the forms which could serve as paradigms.

Can we discern here an extra-musical dimension? There has been no lack of trying and the programmes Mahler wrote, and which he repudiated later on with many regrets, have fostered this misunderstanding. The descriptive intent by itself would be nothing new or characteristic; quite the opposite, it would be typical of an epoch which (after Berlioz and Liszt) liked to stimulate musical perception through images – literary images mainly but also pictures borrowed from the Fine Arts, competing with painting on an inadequate field.

Mahler's extra-musical dimension transgresses these borders and penetrates the very substance of music, its organization, its structure, its capabilities. His vision and his technique have the epic dimension of the narrator: procedures as well as material

Portraits of Gustav Mahler from the period between 1883 and 1903. From left to right: as "Music and Choral Director" of the Cassel Theatre (1883), in Prague (1886), as director of the Royal Opera in Budapest (1888), as principal conductor at the Hamburg Opera House (1891), and as director of the Imperial Opera in Vienna (1903).

ally him above all with the novelist. The word symphony functions mainly as a label. The nomenclature of the movements: Scherzo, slow movement, Finale, is preserved though their number and arrangement change from one work to the other. The occasionally repeated intrusion of the vocal element at various points in the symphony, the use of stage effects by placing some instruments at a distance from the podium

– all that gnaws at the limits of a clearly defined genre. Only the novelist's world possesses enough liberty to permit itself such playing with the material it uses and the manner in which it is used. Released from the visual theatre, his professional obsession, Mahler sometimes throws himself almost maniacally upon this liberty to mix all the genres. He refuses to differentiate between noble and other materials, he mixes all the basic material at his disposal in a construction which, naturally, is carefully controlled but is detached from irrelevant formal limitations. Homogeneity, hierarchy, absurd notions in his case, are disregarded; he transmits to us his vision, including everything there is in it of nobility, triviality, tension, relaxation. There is no choosing among this superabundance, for choosing would end by becoming treason, renunciation of his supreme plan.

So, as listeners, we are exposed to various kinds of perception of the musical flow.

At first hearing the impression persists that the purely musical form is unable to contain such a throng of facts, that the narration – the musical narration, to be sure – gets lost in useless meandering, that the crushing weight destroys the structure, the form dissolves in the multiplicity of layers, that the direction gets lost in episodes which hatch unceasingly, that these overflowing movements must break down due

to the superabundance of material and rhetorical excesses. Purely "musical" listening would support these arguments. How, then, is one supposed to listen? How to perceive? Should one be borne along simply by the narration and let oneself drift according to the psychological fluctuations? Is enjoyment of detail not permitted? Is one to pay attention solely to the epic dimension and to the élan with which it infuses the imagination? Yes, all that is legitimate. This music is powerful enough to carry along even the passive listener; but is that really an advantage? Ideally, one should be able to follow the process of condensation of the narrative.

What has not been said about the lengths of some of Mahler's works? When talking of Schubert we speak of "heavenly lengths", but how can one describe the frightening dimensions of time in certain movements of Mahler's symphonies. Listening to this enormous extension, however, is exhausting and boring only when the perspective is false. (And if this is a problem for the listener it is an even greater one for the interpreter: the only difference being the degree of intensity and preparedness.) The relation to classical architecture with its secure points of view makes no sense; one has to accept the compactness of events, the condensation of musical time which, according to the dramatic situation, is relaxed or dense. Certainly, this elasticity of musical time is the basis of all music but it is not normally the most impressive phenomenon for the perception. With Mahler, there is always an inclination that it will be just so; frequently it controls all the other categories, it guides us and helps to separate what is heard to best advantage as a whole and what must be heard with almost analytical acuteness. The elasticity of musical time enables us to recognize the levels of narration, it immediately helps us to find our way through the thicket of talking sound.

We have to adapt our hearing to the internal organization of the movements, especially when they are huge epic movements; but also inside the symphony itself the individual movements from case to case demand a differentiated listening because their aesthetic conception differs among themselves and because their value, or rather their density, does not have an equal weight at all in the overall organization. Nonhomogeneous as is Mahler's world it accepts the danger of the irreconcilable, embraces quotations and parody as legitimate modes, teaches us once more to listen in a manner that is subtler, more meaningful, richer.

How strange are the extremes hidden in Mahler's work: next to the short lied follows abruptly the overlong symphony. There are no intermediate works. It may seem puzzling... It is possible to value above all the fascinating moments, the immediate, unproblematic perfection, the clearsighted transcription of the text which is

Left: Gustav Mahler in Hamburg in 1897, the year of his appointment to Vienna.

characteristic of his short songs. After the essential has been said, why stretch, why lengthen and enlarge beyond all expectation? And yet – perfect as are these short compositions, Mahler's true dimension lies in the long, hyperbolical, frequently problematic movements, for the difficult struggle with epic amplitude is a more fascinating undertaking than success within dimensions that are all too obviously circumscribed by the boundaries of a clearly established genre. Mahler's attraction would probably be less strong if he were free of his occasional difficulties. His "hypertrophied" manner has very little in common with the pleasure of the *nouveaux riches* in bombast, gigantism and megalomania, it has very little to do with the satiated enjoyment of eccentric luxury; rather, more frequently one suspects the fear of the demiurge calling up from the deep a world that will continue to grow wildly beyond all rational control, the ecstasy of creating a work in which consent and negation weigh equally in the scales, the dissatisfaction with the known dimensions of musical experience, the search for an order less clearly arranged and accepted with less than the customary pleasure. The ideal work refuses all established categories, rejects them as such but participates in all of them. On the crossroads of imaginary theatre, imaginary novel, imaginary poetry, the symphony becomes the meeting place *par excellence*. Musical expression claims all that is usually withheld, it is ready to answer for all the possibilities of existence, it becomes true philosophy and at the same time avoids the rigours of purely verbal communication.

Ambitious projects and economy of means – are they compatible? Is there room in such a concept for an ascesis of sound? We are aware, of course, that limitation and discipline can engender wonderful results, and that the mind, the more it delves into the depths of creation, the less, perhaps, it needs of the external apparatus at its disposal. It refuses the obvious wealth in order to achieve that deepest harmony in which the means of communication become unimportant in the highest degree: material sound handled with absolute mastery is not merely exiled to the most modest spot but receives the most unusual attribute imaginable: non-existence... Music for introspection, books for meditation, song for its own sake – communication taking place beyond the reality of sound. It has been done: by Bach, of course, and almost by Beethoven who paid no attention to the miserable fiddle. Wagner, on the other hand, enjoys even in the deepest regions of his mind the luxuriant sound, the instrumental wealth; purified, filtered, transparent, it is still present even there; subliminal, powerful, this pleasure is, so to speak, the sine of the arc for the essence of expression. How could one overlook such an example, an amalgam, a fusion within the musical thinking, the concept, the means!

Gustav Mahler on the way to the Opera in 1904.

The means – have they not acquired an unbecoming position in relation to the concept? Does not Mahler push his ability until it becomes abuse, does he not thus fall into the trap of seductive, empty virtuosity? The contemporary reactions to his work practically all take this line: they praise or criticize the virtuosity or the bizarreness; there is no doubt of his dexterity and skill; but he is accused of covering up the lack of content, of distracting the attention of the listener with tricks, of diverting musical perception with superficial and on the whole unnecessary categories. And Mahler the conductor, does he not also suffer from the fault which is the litmus test for the interpreter: to hide through manipulation the absence of originality in his concepts or, at the very least, their weakness, while at the same time the *métier* gives him in an almost scandalous measure access to all the mysteries of such manipulation? One holds it against this hybrid race that it understands all too well the art of manoeuvring one accuses it frequently of cheating, even of treachery.

Gustav Mahler in 1909 as director of the New York Philharmonic Society and guest conductor of the Metropolitan Opera, and (right) as guest conductor of the Concertgebouw Orchestra in Amsterdam.

Indeed, there is virtuosity of sound in Mahler; always obvious though not distracting; even where the conventional is not avoided the stops of inspiration are pulled out in a brilliant way. No doubt it is a link in a precisely known chain of historical perspective and explores – if one wants to be extremely rigorous – no com-

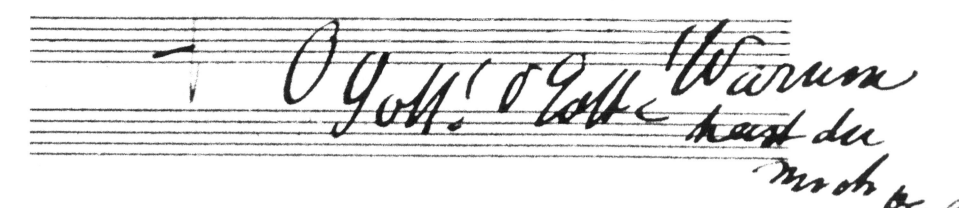

pletely virgin territory; it accepts – and if only to transgress – romantic practices of instrumentation which little by little had become conventions, norms of the 19th century: alone the preference for the horn would suffice to attest to this had there not been other indications. The facility in the instrumental manipulation is so great that one could mistake it sometimes for nonchalance were it not for the fact that the painstaking attention to detail in the writing constantly warns us of such an error. Not without reason is Mahler actually obsessed with the accurateness of his notation; as a conductor he had ample occasion to observe how "liberally" the markings were read and rendered by the instrumentalists, how frequently they were simply ignored – from simple lack of interest or laziness. In his notation he fights to the best of his ability against passive resistance and against traditional habits, those reactions which by the mechanism of the mind had become "natural" and which he distrusts. Knowing himself well, being fully aware of the occasional multifaceted ambiguity of his musical material, unavoidably so since he moved in the uncertain realm between irony and sentimentality, he warns ceaselessly, calls indefatigably to order. One cannot miss his voice in the many positive as well as negative instructions: he incites and holds back, he urges on and applies the brakes, he stimulates impulse and rouses the critical sense. What one has to do is, first of all, to know what one must not do – the expected quality is achieved primarily through the avoiding of mistakes. Actually, he is imbedding the model of the interpreter into the model of the composition, and that to an extent no composer before his time had done; he incorporates the demands of the interpreter with the stream of invention without, however, being tyrannized by them, for he is so much their master that he cannot be satisfied with the existing but anticipates what enlarging and enhancing could possibly achieve. That, not some empty virtuosity, is the mark of the professional interpreter, the man who had daily contact with the masterworks of an inspiring *métier*, but also with the painstaking tasks and obligations of a constricting technique. But to infer from this that the demands of the score would result in a strict execution of all the markings; that living authority would posthumously become rigid compulsion; that exactitude and correctness sufficed to cope with a mind that dwelt near the extremes; that objective obedience to rules could take the place of the enjoyment in a mighty subjectivity – to believe these things creates the immeasurable gap which submissive devotion without imagination is unable to bridge. If Mahler put up warning signs for his interpreter he did not mean to fence him in; from all that is known about him he was not unaware of this tendency of fencing-in, quite the contrary, but he was not ready to accept sloppiness for "interpretation": the most demanding freedom actually requires the strictest discipline, otherwise it becomes a caricature and is satisfied with approximations – with sometimes gross travesties of an otherwise profound, respectable truth. The more one gives in to imprudent ecstasy, even in the hysteria of the moment, the more the original motivation is disturbed. One destroys the multilayered ambiguity which is the essence of this music – in so doing one makes it uncommonly trivial and squanders its deep content; what is more, one hurts the subliminal structure which keeps all the moments of development in balance; one permits this development to degenerate into the confused, chaotic, disoriented motions of an oaf! Mahler's magnetic fields are immensely more sophisticated than the coarse iron filings of an experiment.

The difficulty for Mahler's "reader" is unquestionably caused by the split between gesture and material; the gesture is inclined to become ever more "grandiose", whereas the material is in danger of sliding down ever deeper into "vulgarity". The lack of cohesion is engendered just as much by this fundamental contradiction as by the impossibility of joining together the multiple impulses of his state of mind within the composition. This attitude results in an overgrowth of the musical ideas around some basic poles. The deeper one enters into Mahler's work the clearer the fact of the texture gaining in density becomes, and this not by swelling but by a multiplicity of lines: polyphony develops through an uninterrupted, continuous crisscrossing during which the elements acquire an increasingly strong context with a determining pattern of themes: there is no filling or surrogate matter, all there is are cells which derive from the principal figures. The attention to detail and the grandeur of the project must match – to accomplish it is not easy, but it repairs the unstable balance of the forces which were at work in Mahler's creation. The difficulty of getting hold of these contradictory dimensions, of making them congruent by applying the same perspective, posed the same problems for Mahler as it does for us; these are problems which reveal the deepest, most personal character of his creation.

Gustav Mahler in 1906, in Vienna.

März 1906

That such a work needed time before it became convincing does not seem unreasonable today. The exuberance and the lushness are more attractive now than in former times, they call back to memory the luxuriance which for many years had been forgotten or damned as superfluous and lascivious. But this somewhat primitive reaction would not in itself suffice to explain the attraction which has established itself more and more towards a work that had first been repudiated because of its ambiguity but whose very ambiguity establishes its value today. To link it with a progressive movement which at once and easily leads us to the Vienna school would be to violate the facts and make them say something of which they are incapable. There is too much nostalgia at work, too much contact with the past to enable one to construct in good faith a revolutionary who unleashed an irreversible process of radical innovation. His first followers, principally aware of the nostalgia, noticed this quite clearly: they saw the sentimental aspect and refuted the critical side which made them feel uneasy. On the other hand an unyielding effort to get rid of the categories of the past exists, to force them to say things which originally lay outside their province, with borders so persistently stretched out that Mahler cannot be narrowly claimed as "the end product of a line of generations". In a very personal way he is part of the future: we believe we can recognize this part today more definitely since the stylistic ideas of his work and his time have been sublimated to a certain degree and since we are today ready to accept a more artificially constructed language, a more complex expression, a more obvious synthesis. No doubt, the sources of his inspiration, even the geography of these sources, may seem strictly limited to us, locked up in a world which – far removed from any renovation – remains stubbornly fixed on certain norms of expression, reflexes of a social system which is inevitably wilting away. Since those sources hardly exist any longer we can regard them benignly, as valuable testimonies which we cannot understand any longer directly. This material has taken on documentary value and instead of refuting it we prefer to look at it as the first step of invention. That makes it possible to give our attention from there on almost exclusively to its transformation and transmutation. Throughout the whole work we perceive the development of expression from identical basic elements which serve as indispensable points of reference. The breadth and complexity of the gesture, just as the variety and intensity of the *steps* of the invention – this is what brings Mahler up-to-date; this makes him essential for today's thinking about the future of music.

(Translated from the German by Albrecht Joseph)

Gustav Mahler in 1907, in Vienna.

"He never found deliverance in his agonized effort to find sense in human life. He was distracted by ardent activity; he was helped by his humour to cast off the burden. A vivid concern about intellectual questions strengthened him and helped to still a really unquenchable thirst for knowledge and comprehension. Yet his spirit never knew escape from the torturing question: For what? It was the driving impulse of his every activity."

BRUNO WALTER

Gustav Mahler's death mask, taken by Carl Moll. Right: Replica of the bust by Rodin dating from 1911, now in Paris.

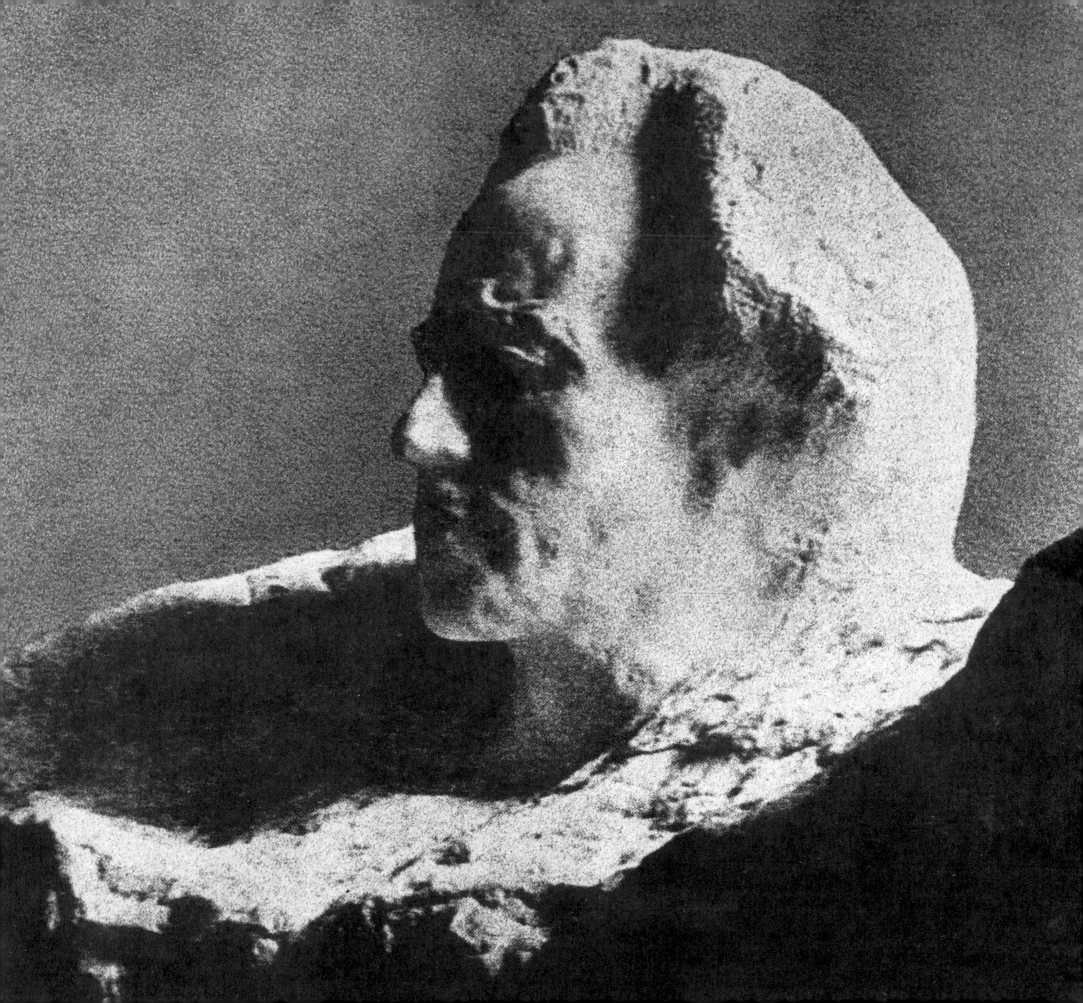

Hilde Spiel

THE VIENNA OF GUSTAV MAHLER

How can one explain the undreamt-of concentration, the profusion and colour in all aspects of art in Vienna at the turn of the century? What was the source of all those profound insights, those flashes of illumination in the field of psychology during that astonishing era?

Attempts have been made to discover the reasons for this from many points of view and in the most varied connections, but whether one proceeds from a historical, sociological, ideological or from a purely phenomenological basis, one always uncovers the same root.

It is quite sufficient to name just a few of those whose reflected glory lent lustre to a period lasting from about 1890 until the outbreak of the First World War. Freud, Otto Weininger, Schnitzler, Hofmannsthal, Beer-Hofmann, Peter Altenberg, Mahler, Schönberg, Richard Gerstl, Karl Kraus, not to mention Herzl, the mediocre dramatist who was nonetheless the visionary founder of a state – there was hardly one of them whose family actually came from the Imperial capital, not one who could have stayed in it after March 1938.

What conclusions can be drawn from this? By the end of the century one particular group – until recently outlawed – from among the mixture of races which made up

The Kärtnerstraße in Vienna at the turn of the century. Left: In the foreground, the opera house; in the background the tower of St. Stephen's cathedral.
Above: Staircase, landing and lift door in a middle-class house in Vienna (Linke Wienzeile 40) built by Otto Wagner.

33

A court ball. In the centre is the Emperor Franz Joseph. This watercolour by Gause dates from 1900.

the old Habsburg monarchy had reached a degree of emancipation, of social freedom and of cultural refinement which allowed it to crystallize the Austrian emotion, the Austrian spiritual attitude, the Austrian taste for art – perhaps even to personify it.

In a century in which everywhere in Europe the function of patronage was shifting away from the upper strata of society to the social middle class, this group had be-

34

Der erste Mai in Wien.
Die Arbeiter marschiren über die Aspernbrücke in den Prater.

The First of May in Vienna. From the *Illustriertes Wiener Extrablatt* of 4 May 1890. In that year, for the first time, the Vienna working class celebrated 1 May; it had been declared a public holiday by the First International.

come, moreover, the most important receptacle of literary, musical and artistic creations. The bourgeoisie, which in England and France had for a long time been the backbone of the state, was almost non-existent in Austria – at least prior to the March Revolution of 1848. Apart from the short period of Vienna's imperial freedom in the Middle Ages, towns owing sole allegiance to the Emperor had not even existed

35

Above: Karl Lueger, mayor of Vienna from 1897 to 1910. He was the founder of the Christian Social Party which represented the urban working class and which, in 1907, became the strongest party in parliament. Right: View of Vienna in 1873, by Gustav Veith; (left foreground) the opera house and (below, right) at the Belvedere Park, the Rennweg with Mahler's house (corner of the Auenbruggergasse).

and therefore no self-confident patriciate had emerged in this country. Up to the beginning of the 19th century and the ascent of the merchant and trading profession, a servile, almost flunkey-like mentality prevailed among the masses. The promotion of the arts was in the hands of the aristocracy and the petty nobility descended from army officers and civil servants – by no means always the best people for the job. Fanny von Arnstein, a Jewish lady raised to the rank of baroness, founded the first literary salon in Vienna as long ago as 1780 – a "bureau d'esprit" as it was called, where the evenings were not "yawned away with the wretched rustling of cards" as was the custom in the great houses.

The tradition was carried on. Fanny's daughter, Baroness Henriette Pereira-Arnstein, received the beaux esprits of the city during the Biedermeier period. It was Frau Josephine von Wertheimstein – according to the Paris *Revue des deux Mondes* the "poetess-queen" of Viennese society – whose warmth and subtle appreciation of art caused the painters, musicians and poets of Vienna, as well as such learned people as the physiologist Ernst von Fleischl, who became the mentor of Sigmund Freud, to come under her spell in the seventies.

All of them, important and much-admired women, were tainted with the "blemish" of Jewry which existed in the eyes of many citizens in spite of its having obtained the "unqualified, complete and fundamental equality of rights" in 1867.

Nevertheless, the liberal era had swept away most of the prejudices and together with the increasing prosperity and the rising social importance of the Jewish bourgeoisie, the talents, indeed the geniuses, among its ranks multiplied.

In the salon of Frau von Wertheimstein, as in that of her sister Sophie von Todesco, "Loris" (the young Hugo von Hofmannsthal) read his first poems and lyric dramas. And when the "old lady of Döbling", whom he deeply venerated, died in July 1894, he was moved to write the "Tercet on Impermanence", the best verses of his early years.

Around 1890, while still at grammar school, Loris was taken up by that circle of writers which has left its mark on literary history under the name of *Jung Wien* ("Young Vienna"). Among its members were Arthur Schnitzler, Richard Beer-Hofmann, Leopold von Andrian, Hermann Bahr and Felix Dörmann; and whenever, as was their custom, they met in the Café Griensteidl in the Herrengasse, Karl Kraus the journalist sat not far away. His battle against the *Journaille* had not yet begun. In 1897, when their regular café was demolished, Karl Kraus came into prominence for the first time as an aggressive pamphleteer and his satirical work was directed at the writers who used to sit at the next table. His "The Demolished Literature"

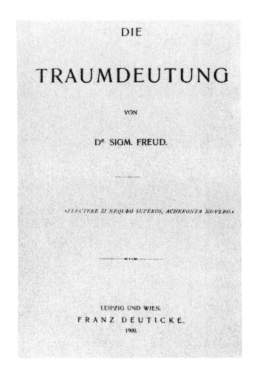

Title pages of the first editions. The two works signalled the start of a new era.

38

was the polemic of a Jew who spared no one of the same ancestry, among them Schnitzler, Hofmannsthal and Beer-Hofmann: this was the best possible proof that the merger with the rest of the population was complete.

For more than a generation, Kraus, the severest critic and arbiter of tastes and morals in Vienna over a period of time which began in 1897 and ended with his death in 1936, was a leading figure in all aspects of aesthetics. In this capacity he vehemently supported Adolf Loos, the architect, in his fight against ornamentation which was becoming ever more rigorously propagated by those visual artists who, in that same significant year of 1897, had deserted the academic school of painting. He favoured Loos's demands for bare façades, ascetic lines, cubist building elements, but using the noblest of materials. He was against the decorative excesses of the Secession, against its climbing creepers, shiny gold spirals, colourfully patterned lamps, textiles and wallpapers, sumptuous utility articles; in short, he was against *art nouveau* which, with the help of Gustav Klimt, Josef Hoffmann and the *Wiener Werkstätte,* controlled the direction in which Viennese art was moving.

"I'll shave off the beards and sweep away the ornaments!" – this was the famous sentence with which Kraus ended a carping article on the subject. A clever man once explained away the hate which Kraus and Loos felt for ornament as being a reaction to a secret fear of castration. But this is delving into an area of depth psychology which should not be touched upon here. Certainly Kraus was not unaffected by the fact that Hermann Bahr, a man whom he totally rejected, was one of those in the van of the Secessionist movement. Their real spokesman, their ideologist, was Ludwig Hevesi from Budapest, who was responsible for the motto "To every age its art, to art its freedom" – perpetuated in stone by J. M. Olbrich on the Secession building.

Moses had forbidden his people to indulge in idolatry, and indeed they have always been less productive in the visual arts than in the art of language. Even though there was hardly a Jewish painter, artist-craftsman, sculptor or architect among the Secessionists, they were heavily patronized by other members of the same faith. Apart from Hevesi, whose book *Eight Years of Secession* described the most active and fruitful years of the movement, the industrialist Fritz Wärndorfer had done more than anyone else to promote the Secessionists' influence on daily life. It was Wärndorfer who, with generous sums of money, financed that eminent school of commercial art and interior decoration founded by Josef Hoffmann and modelled on English prototypes, the *Wiener Werkstätte.* And Wärndorfer himself came to grief over the most ambitious projects of the *Wiener Werkstätte,* above all the fantastic showpiece produced by Hoffmann, Klimt, Kolo Moser, C. O. Czeschka and many other artists:

the Palais Stoclet near Brussels which finally used up all the resources of the workshops.

Gustav Klimt, acknowledged head of the Secession, found his most ardent admirers and keenest clients in the prosperous and emancipated middle classes. The portraits of Adele Bloch-Bauer, Serena Lederer and Margaret Stonborough-Wittgenstein, sister of the philosopher, were among his most masterly representations of soulful, esoteric and at the same time eminently Viennese femininity. Certainly he himself chose to ignore the only Jewish genius among the Viennese painters – or was ignored by him; in 1907 Richard Gerstl declined to allow his works to be exhibited together with Klimt's famous *University Pictures* – perhaps more out of reticence than from disdain. A year later, following an unhappy love affair with Schönberg's first wife, he took his own life.

Gerstl's passion for Mahler's music is well-known. Even after Gerstl had become friendly with Schönberg and Alexander von Zemlinsky, Mahler's music continued to exert a lasting and undiminishing influence on him. But there were other, far closer connections between Mahler and the visual arts. Through his wife, the daughter of the outstanding plein-air painter, Emil Jakob Schindler, and stepdaughter of the Se-

The Michaelerplatz in 1883, a watercolour by Rudolf Alt. Above: Detail of the Post Office Savings Bank in Vienna, built by Otto Wagner with a view of the former War Ministry. Wagner's building is still quite rightly considered to be the typical example of the beginning of modern architecture.

cessionist Carl Moll, he came into direct contact with the various movements in painting. In May 1902, when an intimate party for Max Klinger was given in the Secession building where his monument to Beethoven was being exhibited, Mahler conducted an orchestra of wind instruments from the Imperial Opera playing at the request of Moll his own arrangement of the Song of Joy from the *Ninth Symphony*. Alma Mahler-Werfel tells us that "as the bashful Klinger entered the hall, he was choking with emotion and the tears were coursing slowly down his cheeks."

A time of strong emotions, an era of melancholy; the inherited gloominess of all Jewry – "the weariness of long-forgotten peoples", as Loris called it – combined with a tendency to dejection, to taedium vitae, to capricious ill-temper which affected the most sensitive and the most gifted Viennese. This was further nourished by the mood of impending doom which was steadily gaining ground in spite of the assumed air of high spirits prevailing during the last years of the Habsburg Empire. Two related dispositions met here at the right moment in history. Nowhere is that wistful attitude of mind, that climate of suffering, of futility and inner strife more clearly expressed than in the music of Gustav Mahler. It was significant that, amidst all the sadness, the music had to retain a light, popular element. Ernest Jones, Freud's biographer, reveals the origin of this compunction in his book.

Mahler had consulted the great explorer of the unconscious in August 1910 because his marriage to Alma had reached a crisis. Jones writes on that point: "In the course of the talk Mahler suddenly said that now he understood why his music had always been prevented from achieving the highest rank through the noblest passages, those inspired by the most profound emotions, being spoilt by the intrusion of some commonplace melody. His father, apparently a brutal person, treated his wife very badly, and when Mahler was a young boy there was a specially painful scene between them. It became quite unbearable to the boy, who rushed away from the house. At that moment, however, a hurdy-gurdy in the street was grinding out the popular Viennese air 'Ach, du lieber Augustin'. In Mahler's opinion the conjunction of high tragedy and light amusement was from then on inextricably fixed in his mind, and the one mood inevitably brought the other with it."

Jones, of course, could not know that this paradox was an intrinsic part of this historic street-ballad; indeed it is the earliest example of laughing despair, of the macabre gaiety inherent in the native Viennese character. In 1679, accompanied by the cheerful sounds of the refrain, "Alles ist hin" ('Everything's gone'), Augustin the bagpiper came to life out of a plague hole and even today the Heurigen singers (Austrian singers who come to the taverns when the first new wine is drunk) give a lusty

The famous statue of Beethoven by Max Klinger was shown at the fourteenth exhibition of the *Vereinigung bildender Künstler Österreichs (Secession)*. Gustav Mahler also took an active part in this exhibition (April – June 1902) where important works by Gustav Klimt and Josef Hoffmann were also on show. At the opening ceremony Mahler conducted his own arrangement for brass instruments of the Finale of Beethoven's *Choral Symphony*.
Left: The exhibition poster designed by Alfred Roller.
Right: The *Secession* building in Vienna – a sketch by Joseph Maria Olbrich, the architect of the exhibition building erected in 1897/98.

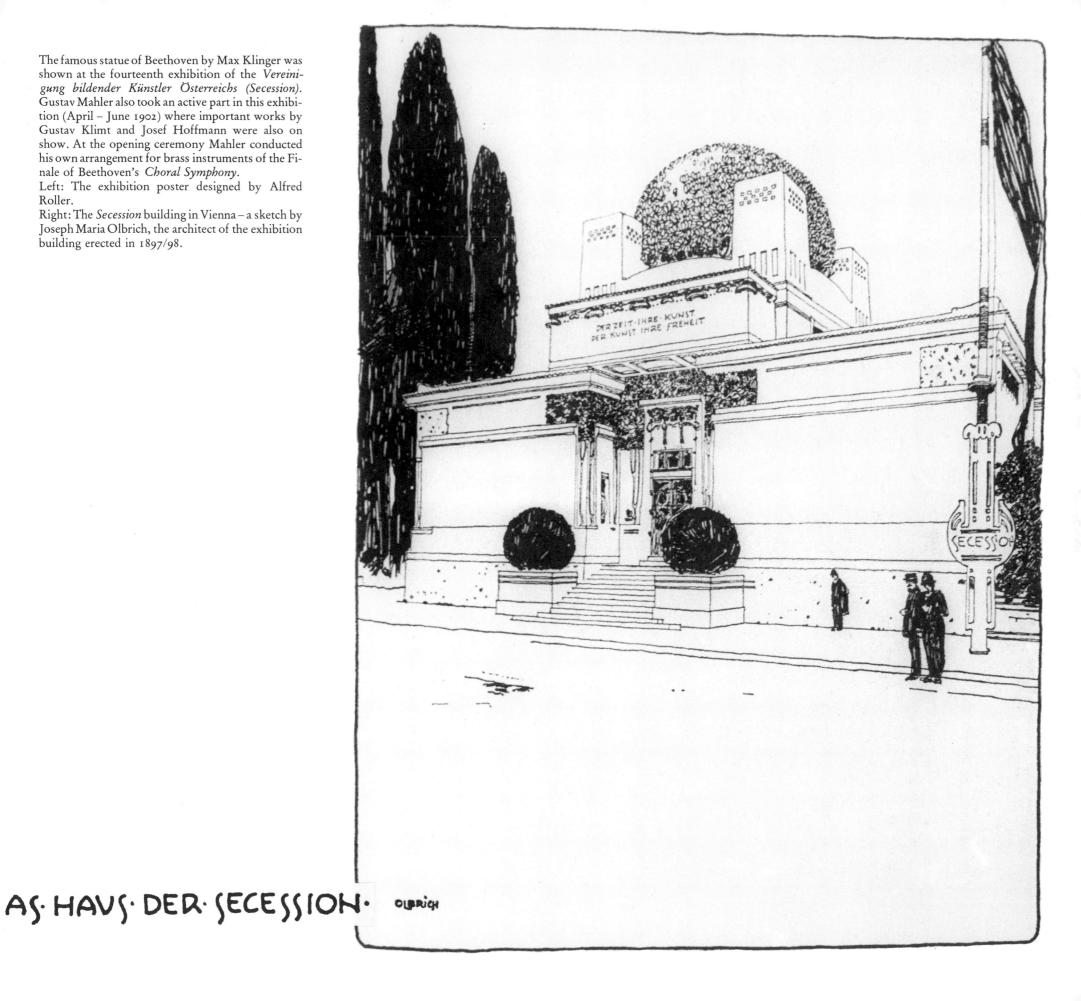

DAS·HAUS·DER·SECESSION·   OLBRICH

Vignette by Alfred Roller to a poem by Ernst Schur (from the *Ver Sacrum*, 1900). Right: Detail of the façade of the Engel Apotheke (pharmacy) in the Bognergasse, Vienna, designed by Oscar Laske, a pupil of Otto Wagner.

rendering of such lines as "When one day I shall die" in three-four time. While still living in the small Moravian town of Jihlava, Gustav Mahler was affected by this Viennese characteristic. Arthur Schnitzler, who was born of Hungarian parents in the capital, was the first person to describe this "infection" and the figures he conjured up – the deeply sad "sweet girl", the languid *femme fatale*, Anatol the world-weary seducer – were all personifications of the Viennese way of life distilled from the abundance of existing models.

Eros and Thanatos – those two primordial forces posited by Sigmund Freud, the interaction of which is probably most clearly discernible in the Vienna of the time, and for that reason could not have been found anywhere else – are to be found all through the works of Arthur Schnitzler. In his famous letter to Schnitzler of May 1922, Freud wrote that he had gained the impression that "you, through your intuition – strictly speaking through meticulous self-perception – have all the knowledge I have laid bare in my painstaking work with other people. It is my firm belief that deep within you lies a psychological explorer who delves into the depths of man's soul – as honest, as impartial and intrepid as anyone who ever lived." Schnitzler had tracked down within himself an accurate comprehension of the state of the soul of the Viennese – knowledge which Freud, born like Mahler in a Moravian village, only acquired during the latter course of his life.

Here the circle closes, the ground covered by this book is circumscribed; the cultural life in Vienna at about the time when Mahler was working at the Imperial Opera, from the end of the century until far into the first decade of the next. Just as in Schnitzler's *Reigen*, the greatest representatives of this cultural life joined hands with each other. This is hardly surprising since most of them came from the same social stratum – the same milieu – and had reached the same level of education. Mahler seems to have grown out of this ambience quite naturally and to have joined the ranks of the exponents of literature, art, music and science of the age. This in no way detracts from his greatness nor does it belittle the genius of Schnitzler, Gerstl, Schönberg or Freud if one explains it on the basis of local factors and genetic premisses.

This extraordinarily prolific fusion of Jewish intellect and emotion at the peak of its refinement with the Viennese character – a product of a centuries-old multi-national, multi-ethnic, multi-lingual past – received its *coup de grâce* in 1918, though it did not end abruptly. Its influence continued to be felt during the twenties and thirties. Only with the emergence of the Third Reich was the fruitful union annihilated, never again to bear a yield of such splendour and opulence.

Right: In the Café Griensteidl (watercolour by Reinhold Völkel). The Café on the Michaelerplatz, also called the "Café Größenwahn" ("Café Megalomania") was the centre of Viennese literary life up to 1896. When it was closed, Karl Kraus wrote *The Demolished Literature* and the writers, greater and lesser, moved into the Café Central.

Henry-Louis de La Grange

GUSTAV MAHLER'S ROADS TO VIENNA

Gustav Mahler's impressions of Vienna when he saw the capital for the first time – on a day in the early autumn of 1875 – could scarcely have been anything less than ecstatic. A sensitive 15-year-old, fresh from the small Moravian town of Iglau (Jihlava), where his parents had been living since he was six months old, he found himself at the heart of the world of European music. He knew that no other city could offer him a better chance of becoming a skilled musician, so he had done his very best to show off his talents to one of Vienna's most influential piano teachers, Julius Epstein. Only Epstein was capable of persuading his father to let him go. The elder Mahler watched and waited. And, by the grace of God, Gustav succeeded: "Herr Mahler, your son is a born musician," Epstein declared, emphasizing the fact in a clever pun on Bernhard Mahler's trade as a distiller: "This young man has spirit, but he won't be taking over his father's spirit business!"

Thus Gustav Mahler enrolled at the Vienna Conservatory in September and took up quarters in the beautiful, frivolous, cosmopolitan city he had dreamt of for so long. During his three years at the Conservatory, Mahler's very modest circumstances prohibited indulgence in many of the pleasures Vienna had to offer. He was compelled to survive on a meagre allowance from his father and what he could earn

Gustav Mahler's registration form after his marriage in 1902. Left: Walking on the Ringstraße. After a watercolour by Theo Zasche. Among the walkers are Gustav Mahler and Arnold Rosé (right, in the foreground), members of the Opera such as Selma Kurz, Willi Hesch, Leo Slezak and Fritz Schrödter, some journalists, officials and "high society".

Gustav Mahler in Iglau, 1872. Right: Mahler's course of study at the Conservatory for the 1876/77 school year. Opposite: Detail of the *Musikverein* building in Vienna, built by Theophil Hansen between 1867 and 1870. The building became the focal point of concert life in Vienna. For many years the Conservatory was also housed in this building.

from giving an ill–paid piano lesson now and then. Yet despite the fact that he could afford very few visits to concert halls or the Opera House, he was still profoundly influenced and stimulated by the warm, carefree atmosphere of this great Central European metropolis, the adopted home of Mozart and Beethoven – two of his favourite "masters", whose steps the young Mahler, always an inveterate lover of Sunday walks, enjoyed retracing through Wieden, Grinzing, Nussdorf and Heiligenstadt. During his Conservatory years, Mahler's musical vocation was confirmed, but he also discovered the delights of Viennese popular music: the Ländler, the waltzes and the *Schrammelmusik* which were to play such an important role in his mature style, along with the military music which had delighted his childhood.

Mahler's teachers – apart from Julius Epstein (piano) – were Franz Krenn (counterpoint and composition) and Robert Fuchs (harmony), strongly conservative musicians who had achieved a certain reputation, one as a liturgical composer, the other as the composer of several string serenades. Both were no doubt shocked by the "eccentricities" and the loose, "Wagnerian", style of young Mahler's music. They should be given credit for teaching him the basic discipline of composition, beautifully demonstrated by the traditional, even Brahmsian, style of his early *Piano Quartet*. Their tutelage helped him to win first prizes in composition at the end of his first and last years at the Conservatory.

Mahler's early compositions have frequently been listed, although nothing has survived except a couple of lieder fragments and a complete piano-quartet movement followed by the opening bars of another. Among the works that have disappeared are an uncompleted opera, *Ernst von Schwaben*, composed mainly when he was living in Iglau, and two or three orchestral works (including the often cited *Nordische Symphonie*), a group of chamber works, a few lieder and possibly some piano pieces. A number of these may have been partly improvised and partly played from memory, since he later conceded that he left most of his student works unfinished. It should be noted that he became an accomplished and even brilliant pianist at the Conservatory, but that he did not study conducting there. The school's records show that he was an unruly student. Some of his teachers and classmates found him "arrogant" and coldly ambitious, though others liked him intensely and found him a "genius". He often clashed with the school authorities, since he never bothered to conceal that he had a mind of his own. He always avoided the worst, however, and he was never expelled – like Hugo Wolf, his close friend. His other classmates included Felix Mottl, founder of the school's very active Wagnerverein and later a famous conductor; Arnold Rosé, who married one of Mahler's sisters and spent half

Above: The house in Kalischt (Bohemia) where Gustav Mahler was born.
Right: Mahler's application for leave (undated) to the Director of the Conservatory, Professor Hellmesberger. Mahler's professor, Julius Epstein, recommends acceptance.

a century as Kapellmeister of the Vienna Philharmonic; Rudolf Krzyzanowski, who achieved a certain renown as a conductor; and Hans Rott, a gifted and original composer who the young Mahler felt was more talented than he himself.

As an early member of the Wagnerverein, Mahler undoubtedly attended the Vienna performances of *Tannhäuser* and *Lohengrin* which Richter conducted in the composer's presence in December 1875 and January 1876. He heard Epstein play the Schubert *Sonatas* he had practised under his teacher's guidance, as well as the Brahms *Piano Quartets* (with the Hellmesberger Quartet). He also attended piano recitals given by Franz Liszt and Anton Rubinstein. Since he rarely had enough money to spend on seats at the Opera, he probably learned most operas by studying the scores just before he conducted them for the first time. This perhaps explains why he always found performing "traditions" suspect and frequently ignored them.

Because of his early admiration for the composer of *Tristan*, Mahler was surely looked on as a member of the "Wagnerian" faction in the battle which ranged conservatives (headed by Brahms and the critic Eduard Hanslick) against Bruckner, the "Wagnerian" symphonist, and his pupils. Nevertheless, too much has been made of Mahler's kinship with Bruckner. He did attend his courses at the University later on, though he didn't even bother to claim official academic credit for doing so. Bruckner's influence on his own musical style is, of course, obvious, yet he was never a whole-hearted admirer of the older man's compositions. He conducted them only rarely, and then often in the cut or revised versions so despised by true Brucknerians. What he liked and revered in Bruckner was clearly his innocence, his naïveté and sincerity – even more than he admired his stature as a composer. He revered his works despite what he always considered fatal flaws in their composition.

Nevertheless, one of Mahler's tasks during his last year at the Conservatory was to transcribe Bruckner's *Third Symphony* for piano duet. During these years, his attitude towards another Viennese composer, the more conservative and traditionalist Johannes Brahms, was correspondingly negative. His aversion reached its climax in the year 1880, when Brahms's behaviour towards Hans Rott helped drive Rott into insanity and suicide, and 1881, when the author of the *Deutsches Requiem* was a leading member of the jury which rejected Mahler's *Das klagende Lied*, his first mature composition, when it was proposed for the Beethoven Prize. Later, Mahler's attitude towards Brahms became quite friendly, and Brahms turned into one of the greatest admirers of his conducting. Both Brahms and his friend Hanslick strongly supported Mahler's candidacy for the post of director of the Imperial Opera in 1897.

Mahler ended his second Conservatory year in 1877 with a first prize for his piano playing, passed his "matura" exam in Iglau and enrolled at the University of Vienna to study history, philosophy, philology and literature. Nine months later, he graduated from the Conservatory with another first prize for composition (the Scherzo of a *Piano Quintet*, now lost). The next two seasons in Vienna were perhaps the most troubled and difficult of his entire life. Besides moving incessantly from one noisy flat to another, even noiser, where he found it totally impossible to write or play music, young Mahler was deeply anxious about his future and suffering desperately from two unhappy love affairs.

During these years, along with Wolf and Krzyzanowski, he became an ardent socialist and a vegetarian. The three young men had fallen under the influence of *Religion und Kunst*, an attack on meat-eating launched by Richard Wagner in the wake of his research for *Parsifal*. The socialist group used to get together for dreary meatless meals and non-alcoholic drinks at a Viennese restaurant called Ramharter, at the corner of the Wallnerstrasse and the Fahnengasse. Sometimes Mahler would play the

Deutschlandlied on the restaurant's upright piano. Here he met two young physicians: Albert Spiegler and Victor Adler, a fervent admirer of Nietzsche and Ibsen as well as Wagner; Engelbert Pernerstorfer, the editor of the group's newspaper, *Deutsche Worte;* Heinrich Braun, his brother Otto, and Hans Emmanuel Sax, social theorists; Hermann Bahr, the young writer and a man who became one of Mahler's close friends in later life; Siegfried Lipiner, a young writer and genius "raté" who had been "discovered" by Nietzsche and was proud of it.

Friedrich Eckstein remembered seeing Mahler at the Café Griensteidl too (which the Viennese used to call the "Grössenwahn", or "Megalomania"), on the Michaelerplatz: "He is a short man; his extreme irritability is noticeable in the peculiar unevenness of his walk. His narrow, taut, slender, mobile face is framed by a huge brown beard. His heavily accented speech is precise and has a marked Austrian flavour. He always carries a pile of books or music under his arm and all conversations with him proceed by fits and starts."

Gustav Mahler's house in Hamburg. He became acquainted with Anna von Mildenburg during the years spent there (1891 to 1897). From both the human and artistic point of view, this liaison was of the greatest importance for Mahler.

From June 1883 on, however, anti-Semitic tendencies began to permeate the ideology of these socialist-vegetarians. This is probably why Mahler, who by this time was no longer living in Vienna in any case, finally left the group and started eating meat again. The year 1880 had been a real turning point in his life. Not only did he turn twenty, but he suffered a series of cruel blows: Rott's insanity and suicide, an unhappy love-affair with Josephine Poisl, the daughter of the Iglau postmaster, and the suicide of another girl with whom he had previously been involved. But even at this early age, he was not one of those romantics who derive a morbid pleasure from personal unhappiness. Rather than bewail his fate, he made two major decisions. One was to accept a very modest post as operetta conductor in a small Upper Austrian spa, Bad Hall, near Linz. The other was to finish his first large-scale choral and orchestral work, *Das klagende Lied,* which he would soon submit – but without success – for Vienna's most important competition for new work, the Beethoven Prize.

Detail of the house where Mahler lived in the Auenbrugger-gasse.
Right: View of the entrance hall. Gustav Mahler was officially registered at this address between 1898 and 1909. Although the house was badly damaged in 1945, the façade and staircase remain.

Although Mahler was a success at Bad Hall, an entire year went by before he found another conductor's job, this time at Laibach (Ljubljana) in Slovenia (Northern Yugoslavia), where he made his debut with a genuine, if small, theatre orchestra on 24 September 1881. He conducted operas and operettas there until the end of March 1882. For the second time, he spent the summer in the country near Budapest, where he tutored the children of a rich family. At the end of September he was back in Vienna again – for three more unhappy, destitute months. This time, however, he was firmly resolved to take the first conducting job that came his way. During the closing months of 1882, he worked steadily on the first act of *Rübezahl* (an opera he never finished: the subject had been suggested by Hugo Wolf, who planned to compose it himself and never forgave Mahler for "stealing" his idea). During these same months, Mahler again moved no less than five times, since every time he was in the mood for composing, a crying baby or a piano-playing neighbour would drive the inspiration away. It is conceivable that Mahler already knew, in his innermost heart, that his future as composer did not lie in opera.

The year 1883 brought another turning point. He accepted a two-months' conducting job at Olmütz (Olomouc) in Moravia. In May, acting as chorus master for an Italian opera season at the Carltheater, he heard that his worst difficulties were over. He was offered a post as Kapellmeister at the Kassel Theatre in September.

The following summer was divided between his family at Iglau and Perchtoldsdorf, on the outskirts of Vienna, where his friend the philologist Fritz Löhr lived in a small house overlooking the Marktplatz. Later Löhr remembered how Mahler played Beethoven's Sonata Opus 111, as well as Fugues from Bach's *Well-tempered Clavichord* (and even the complete *Missa Solemnis*). He performed with such brilliance and feeling that enthralled passers-by clustered outside the window.

For the next fourteen years, Mahler returned to Vienna only when he was on his way to and from Iglau, sometimes to visit his impresario, Gustav Löwy, when he was out of a job, sometimes to visit the Löhrs in Perchtoldsdorf. It was in Vienna, at the end of September 1888, that he came to meet Baron Franz von Beniczky, the Intendant of the Budapest Opera, to discuss his appointment as its director. He spent the summer of 1890, together with his brothers and sisters and the Löhrs, in Hinterbrühl, south of Vienna, where he composed a lied with piano accompaniment to a *Wunderhorn* text, now unidentified. He went to Iglau only once, to sell his father's business and the family house left vacant by his parents' death in 1889. Before returning to Budapest, he rented an apartment in Vienna near the Löhrs' so that his brothers and sisters would have a place to live while they continued their studies.

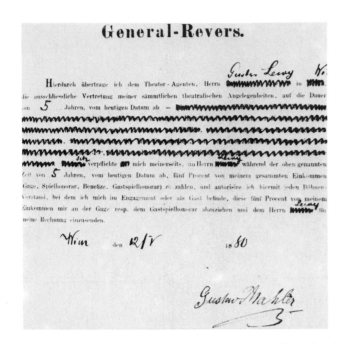

A contract completed and signed by Gustav Mahler (dated 1880) for a period of five years, against five percent of the honorarium. The Gustav Lewy agency was one of the leading agencies at the time; it represented numerous composers, among them Johann Strauss.

In 1891, after leaving the Budapest Opera for that of Hamburg, Mahler once more spent most of June and July in Perchtoldsdorf with his family. But this summer he tired of the climate and the flood of visitors. He decided henceforth he would spend all his summers in the country. From 1893 on, he went to Steinbach, a small resort on the edge of the Attersee, where he wrote the *Second* and the *Third Symphonies* in the small *Häuschen* or summer house he built there, on the lake shore, where he could compose in undisturbed solitude. During his last Hamburg years, the hope of a return to Vienna and an appointment as director of the Imperial Opera became a true obsession. Every month, every week, every day, he waited for the "Call from the God of the Southern Regions," that is, the letter from the Opera authorities, which would open wide the gates of the Austrian capital.

The Giant Wheel at the Vienna Prater in the year in which it was built which was also the year in which Gustav Mahler received his appointment to Vienna. Today the wheel, which was built by an Englishman, Walter B. Basset, is still one of famous Viennese landmarks.

Gottfried Scholz

GUSTAV MAHLER'S SUMMER RETREATS

When at the turn of the century a Viennese citizen fled from the oppressive heat of the city, he did not go away on a journey for his holiday, he went to his summer retreat. This entailed careful planning and called for considerable upheaval. The right spot had to be found and a suitable apartment or house rented before trunks and chests, piano and decorative porcelain objects, cook and children's nurse could be transported by the Austrian railways to the selected destination. The relaxing character of the summer retreat certainly involved a change of surroundings but the manner of living was merely transposed. Many Viennese continued their high-society life "doing nothing" *à la campagne,* and for this they would not be deprived of their close circle of friends, nor did they want to do without the nearness of the *haute volée.* Gustav Mahler, on the other hand, looked for peace in the summer so that he could at last compose undisturbed.

Mahler got to know the countryside of Upper Austria in 1880, at Bad Hall, during the time he was conducting there. The years as Kapellmeister and opera director in Leipzig, Budapest and Hamburg already had shown him to be an industrious, inexorably intellectual worker, who allowed himself only little peace and quiet during the miserably few summer weeks he spent off duty. Conscientiously fulfilling his

Above: Sketch from the *Tenth Symphony.* "Possession of these sketches is the most convenient form of what can be expected of the Tenth; even the first movement can be better praised by reading it in silence than by exposing it in performances in which what is not played, appears of necessity to be incomplete. However, anyone who knows how to differentiate between possibility and reality in music, who knows that the greatest works could have been quite different and greater than they are, will immerse himself in Mahler's handwriting, which is determined and yet born of fear, with the awe that should be accorded to the possible before the actual result. The lovely facsimile almost resembles graphic art." (Theodor W. Adorno, 1969).
Left: Gustav and Alma Mahler walking from Toblach to Altschluderbach during the summer holiday in 1909.

obligations and constantly overworked, he had hardly any opportunity of devoting himself to composition during the season. Mahler finished his *First Symphony* during the period of official mourning for Kaiser William I in 1888, during which the Leipzig Opera House was closed for ten days.

In 1891, after the season in Hamburg ended, he visited Leipzig, Munich and Vienna to outline future plans with friends and patrons. He then went to Perchtoldsdorf to seek peace for a short spell to compose the *Wunderhorn* songs. Thereafter, he visited Marienbad and Bayreuth and subsequently went to Denmark, Norway and Sweden before returning to Hamburg on 21 August. This hectic summer neither calmed his nerves nor gave him any spare time for composition. He decided he would have to make considerable changes in this summer period if he were to continue being a composer of any worth.

This artist, shy of the public and easily upset, sought the loneliness of a summer exile rather than the pleasure of company at a place in the country. The only people whom he tolerated round him were his sisters Justi and Emma, and Natalie Bauer-Lechner, his companion and friend of many years. It is thanks to their diaries that we have many of the details of this part of his life.

Apart from quiet, Mahler above all sought to experience nature; not for him the usual footpaths, but narrow tracks through tangled undergrowth, among the rocks and lonely mountain pastures. The inspiration for his major works came to him in this tranquillity and solitude. He had to be free of all obligations, to be far away from other kinds of music and have people around him who were willing at any time to care for him, faithfully – to serve him almost without intruding and who were not perceptibly affected by his unpredictable reactions.

For Mahler, composing was an elemental experience – not the adaptable work that it was for Richard Strauss. He created the unusual under unusual conditions. Anyone who could be enthusiastic about the product of his creating had to tolerate the manner in which it came into being, had to bow to the will of the composer.

Justi and Natalie discovered a quiet place (Steinbach-am-Attersee, a lake in Upper Austria) and in June 1893, together with Mahler's sister and brother, Emma and Otto, took a small, cheap, five-room apartment with cooking facilities in the "Gasthof zum Höllengebirge". The first real summer of composition began. Important parts of the *Second Symphony* were written in not quite three months as well as some of the *Wunderhorn* songs, among them *St. Anthony of Padua's Sermon to the Fishes*, first imagined on the shores of the lake. The first summer in Steinbach was so successful for the composer that he resolved to make this spot his permanent "exile".

Gustav Mahler's table of themes for the *Third Symphony*.
Right: Gustav and Alma Mahler with their daughters,
Maria and Anna in Maiernigg, 1905.

He commissioned a builder to erect a little cottage on a meadow near the Gasthof so that in future he would be able to devote himself to his work with even less disturbance than before, and by 1894 it was ready. This modest little building consisted of a single room with windows on three sides. Inside there was just room for a table and chairs, a piano and a small stove. He forbade anyone to seek him out there "on pain of death".

Mahler was so allergic to noise that often he could only work with the windows closed. His day's work began at six-thirty. The morning working hours were sacred to him; after a late lunch he went for long walks. His friends who sometimes accompanied him were never astonished if he suddenly became silent in the middle of a conversation, withdrew from them and quickly sketched out new musical ideas.

He began his *Third Symphony* in this idyllic setting. About the origin of the phrase "what the flowers of the field tell me" Natalie observes: "This was the piece that Mahler composed last summer when he had only just come to Steinbach. Straight away, on the first afternoon as he looked out over the meadow from his tiny house completely surrounded by grass and flowers, he outlined it and finished it in one stroke. 'Anyone who does not know the locality', said Mahler, 'could almost imagine, so uniquely charming is it, that it was especially created to provide the impulse for musical inspiration.'" When Bruno Walter once visited him and admired the rocky cliffs across the water, Mahler said to him "You don't have to bother to look any more – it is all in my music."

Now and then Mahler interrupted his periods of creative withdrawal to go on extensive cycle tours and to visit friends. Johannes Brahms, who went for relaxation to Bad Ischl, the Imperial summer health resort, gladly received the "King of the Revolutionaries" to discuss the latter's work.

Contacts with important people from the Viennese world of opera were also essential to Mahler. To become director at the Opera House had for years been the objective of his yearnings and plans. He spent the summer of 1896 – his fourth and last in Steinbach – restless and discouraged. The rented piano had not been delivered that year (from then on he dispensed with this "aid to composition"), he had left behind in Hamburg the previous year's outline drafts of the first movement of the *Pan Symphony* and waited restlessly for them to be forwarded. He felt unable to return because he did not like the inn's new owners. He had been composing at Steinbach for four summers and it was with tears in his eyes that he bade farewell to his house. The next year he was restless and troubled. His engagement to Anna von Mildenburg was broken off and the time spent hoping and striving for the directorship of the Vienna Opera was hardly conducive to the germination of composition ideas. Without a permanent summer place, escorted by his usual companions, he roamed North and South Tyrol.

He stayed for a while in Vahrn, near Brixen. Then, just as he returned from a cycle tour through the Pustertal lasting several days, he learnt that on 23 July he was to take over the responsibilities of Director Jahn at the Vienna Opera. His dream had come true with all the splendid and hellish aspects which had always been associated with the office of Opera Director in Vienna. Mahler went to Vienna at once. The burdensome work as administrator of the Vienna Opera and the many evenings he had to spent on the conductor's podium left little time during the year for composing. Moreover, Mahler became ill. Following an operation he spent the summer convalescing in Vahrn in the company of Justi, Natalie and Arnold Rosé. During this period he wrote three *Wunderhorn* songs.

The burdens of the 1898/99 season – in addition to his obligations at the Opera, he also conducted the Philharmonic concerts – left Mahler no chance of a quiet summer. Because of a misunderstanding, his search for relaxation in Laussa, near Losenstein in Upper Austria, ended in small, uncomfortable rooms. In great haste he sought other quarters. The Villa Serti at Aussee seemed to be suitable but Mahler soon became acquainted with the deceptiveness of a health resort that was too well-known. The municipal orchestra, which played on a bandstand in the town centre, made an infernal racket: Mahler found the acoustic burden odious. During his walks – actually more like runs in the country – he was even more pestered by Viennese who stared at him open-mouthed. Since his days in Budapest he had hated this – being stared at "like a wild animal". Despite these disturbances he worked as intensively as possible. He revised the score of the *Third Symphony*, orchestrated *Revelge* and began to write the *Fourth Symphony* during the last ten days of his stay. He had no feeling of contentment. Looking back on his composition output of the three previous summers he compared himself bitterly to a swimmer who takes a few strokes just to convince himself he still knows how to swim.

Nervously exhausted and discouraged, he began the new season in Vienna. The faithful Justi and Natalie started looking for a peaceful spot for the coming year. They found the ideal place at Maiernigg on the Wörthersee. Mahler, who visited it briefly in September, was thrilled with the well-wooded lakeside.

He could hardly wait to flee to his new "exile" after an exhausting series of concerts in Paris with the Vienna Philharmonic Orchestra. Once there, he was filled with enthusiasm for its peacefulness. He immediately had a *Häuschen* (little house) built

Mahler's work hut at Maiernigg am Wörthersee. It was here, between 1900 and 1907 that Mahler wrote his *Fourth, Fifth, Sixth, Seventh* and *Eighth Symphonies*.

on a hill and planned to build a villa near the shore of the lake in the coming year. Meanwhile he and his companions lived in the Villa Antonia. The twenty-minute walk between the little house and the apartment increased the "ideal" remoteness even from the members of his family. Bauer-Lechner remarks: "But you really should see the position, even if only the path to his little house. He is surrounded by all the marvels and terrors of the forest as only someone can be who lives in it from hour to hour. No one can have the same feeling as he has when he has closed his lattice door behind him. Here the peace and security and Dionysiac wonder and delights exceed by far even his beloved little hut at Steinbach. He works here with all four windows wide open and continuously breathes the pure forest air and scents, while in Steinbach he had only been able to keep out the ever obtrusive noise by having double doors and windows."

Soon, however, yelping dogs and gaping walkers began to disturb him again. His acoustic idiosyncrasy sometimes made him wish he were deaf, like Beethoven. Despite such overwrought reactions the first summer at Maiernigg proved to be creatively fruitful. After ten months "hibernation" from composing he went back to his sketches for the *Fourth Symphony* and worked feverishly to finish it. He sat in his little house daily from 7 until 12, and in the afternoons from 4 until 7.

The Villa Mahler was not ready to move into until 1901. His physical activities consisted of swimming, sunbathing, rowing, walking and cycling – this was his compensation for all his creative efforts. Away from any sort of etiquette, the Vienna Opera Director could afford to roam around the district unshaven and jacketless and even to be picked up by the police as a vagabond. When he wasn't actually composing, noise did not bother him so much. On a Sunday walk with Rosé the noise of sundry barrel-organs, military bands, merry-go-rounds, shooting booths and puppet shows intruded upon them from all sides. Mahler commented on the "racket": "There's polyphony for you, that's where I get it from. This is exactly how themes should come from different directions, with distinct rhythms and melodies in music (all else is no more than disguised homophony): except that in the latter the artist must adapt, order and unite them into a harmonious whole." In 1901 he did a great deal of creative work as well. In the space of 14 days he composed seven songs. These were followed by the completed scherzo for the *Fifth Symphony*. In Maiernigg he regained the inner and outward peace which, for the overwrought and overworked man, were a prerequisite for creating his great works.

In the winter of 1902 came the great watershed in Mahler's life. His marriage to Alma Schindler had brought a new intellectual circle of friends. Justi hated her sis-

In 1899 Mahler bought some land in Maiernigg am Wörthersee and built this villa. After 1901 he spent his summer holidays there. After the death of his elder daughter, Maria, (1902–1907), he shunned the house and finally sold it.

ter-in-law, Natalie was deeply wounded for she had built up hopes of a permanent relationship with Mahler. The two of them withdrew from his private life, even as summer companions, and were replaced by his spouse and his mother-in-law. Mahler spent the first summer of their marriage in Maiernigg with Alma, who was expecting her first child. The young wife, who was endowed with artistic taste as well as musical understanding and literary sensitivity, considered the Villa stuffy and the furnishings hideous. For example, in her *Memories of Gustav Mahler* she confessed that she tore down the ornamental pillars of a cupboard and was caught in the act by her husband.

However, the composer did not allow his own daily routine to be disturbed by the new conditions. The cook had to leave his breakfast ready for him in the little house and when he got there he warmed the milk himself on a spirit stove and started work straight away. Later, after a short swim, he had a simple meal followed by a walk of several hours with Alma and after this he was quite ready to go back to his composing. The loving wife bowed to the wishes and moods of this egocentric man just as his sister and Natalie had done; indeed, she helped him by doing some of the copying work on his symphonies herself. The *Fifth* to *Eighth Symphonies* were written during the happy summers up to 1906 spent in Carinthia.

The thrilling start of the *Veni Creator Spiritus* came to him one morning as he was going into his *Häuschen*. Mahler worked on the instrumental improvements during the morning hours in Vienna in the following year. It must have been in-

comprehensible to his family that, as the father of two little girls, he added three *Kindertotenlieder* to the two earlier ones. Did he have a presentiment of personal tragedy in these songs as well as in his *Sixth Symphony*?

The summer of 1907 saw the end of the family's happiness. The elder daughter, Maria, the special favourite of her father's, died of scarlatinal diphtheria. The family's

doctor found out that the completely distraught parents both had heart trouble; Mahler himself had a double valvular defect.

He became aware that he had only a short, gloomy future ahead of him. He fled immediately from Maiernigg, never to return. The first outlines for *Das Lied von der Erde* were written in Schluderbach, in the Tyrol. The theme of the farewell flows into this work with sadness and resignation.

The year 1907 also saw the completion of his Vienna period; Mahler resigned as director and at the end of this terrible year came the road to uncertainty in America. Mahler never felt at home in the United States. Despite having acquired friends quickly and enjoying great success as conductor he was permanently on tour. He never thought of taking a holiday there, consequently during the years in America he returned to Europe every spring. As early as 1908 Alma and her mother had found a large country house near Toblach in South Tyrol which had 11 rooms, 2 verandahs and two bathrooms and was very suitable for the family. A "work" house was erected in the woods, in the middle of mossy and rocky ground, and thus the Mahler family moved into the new quarters with two grand pianos and an upright. Meanwhile Maiernigg had been sold and even Mahler's way of living no longer had anything in common with the Carinthian summers. The constant anxiety about his heart complaint prevented him from undertaking any sport. He avoided any exertion, short walks were interspersed with periods of standing still, resting and feeling his pulse: he even took a pedometer with him. The slightest excitement could result in a heart attack. Mahler only really became a sick man when he knew that he had a congenital heart complaint. Concentrating exclusively on himself inevitably led to estrangement from Alma and when in the summer of 1910 he became aware of this, he sought Sigmund Freud's advice.

During the three summers spent in Toblach, he worked on *Das Lied von der Erde* and the two last Symphonies. The summer sojourn in 1910 was not sufficient to finish the *Tenth Symphony*. He returned to America whence, now mortally ill, he had to be brought back to Vienna: here in his musical homeland he sought a cure, but he found only death.

Over the previous few years Mahler had planned to build a summer residence near the Semmering but he did not live to see it. He hardly ever thought of another little house for working in any more. In a letter to his wife he acknowledged that "Man needs sun and warmth. I shiver when I think of the little house where I used to compose; although I spent the happiest hours of my life there, I probably paid for them with my health." This bitter acknowledgment came late – too late.

The beginning of the Pavillon (summer-house) sketch from *Das Lied von der Erde.*
Left: Gustav Mahler with his daughter Anna in Toblach, 1907.

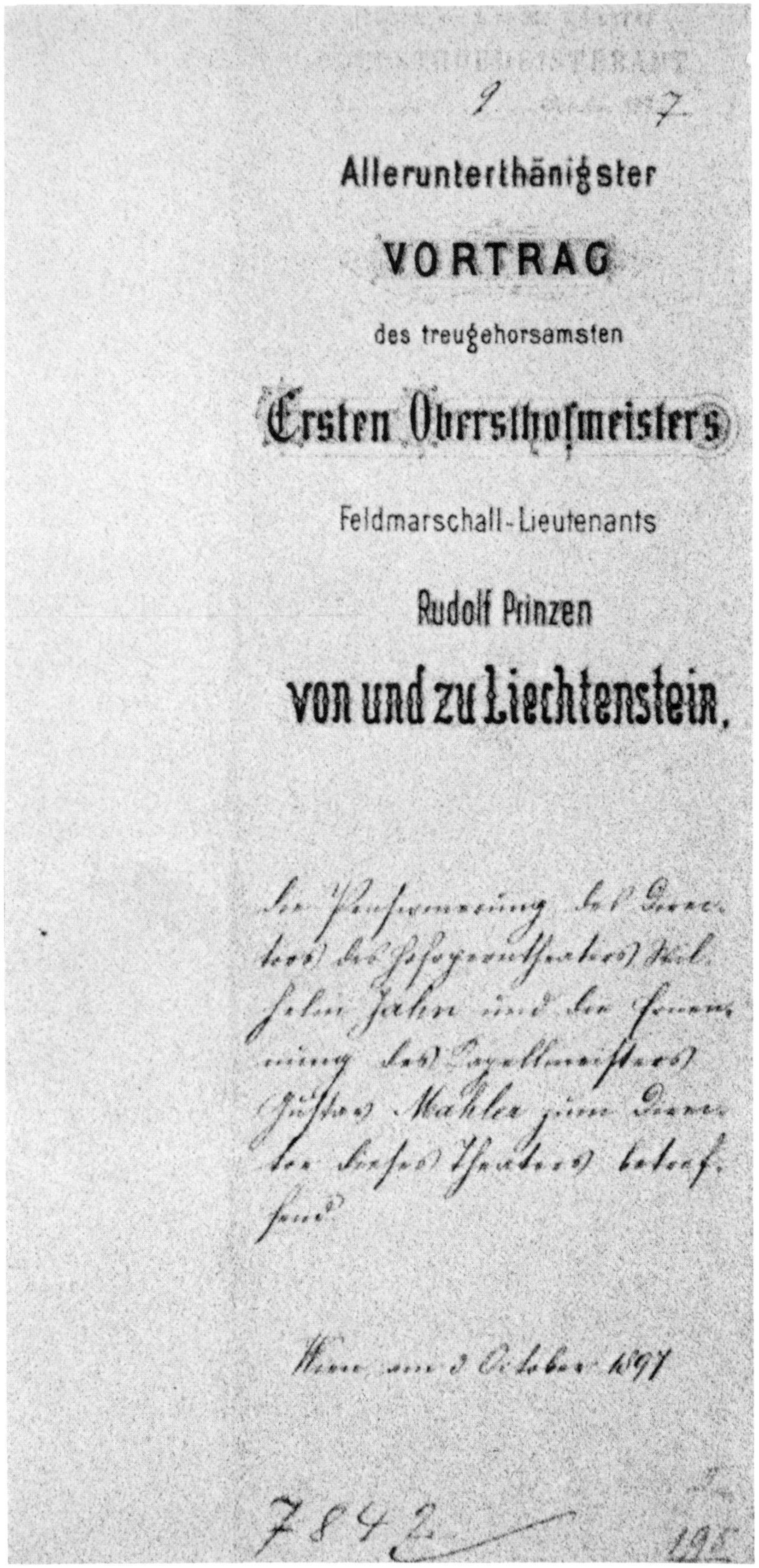

Allerunterthänigster

VORTRAG

des treugehorsamsten

Ersten Obersthofmeisters

Feldmarschall-Lieutenants

Rudolf Prinzen

von und zu Liechtenstein.

Wien am 3 October 1897

7842

195

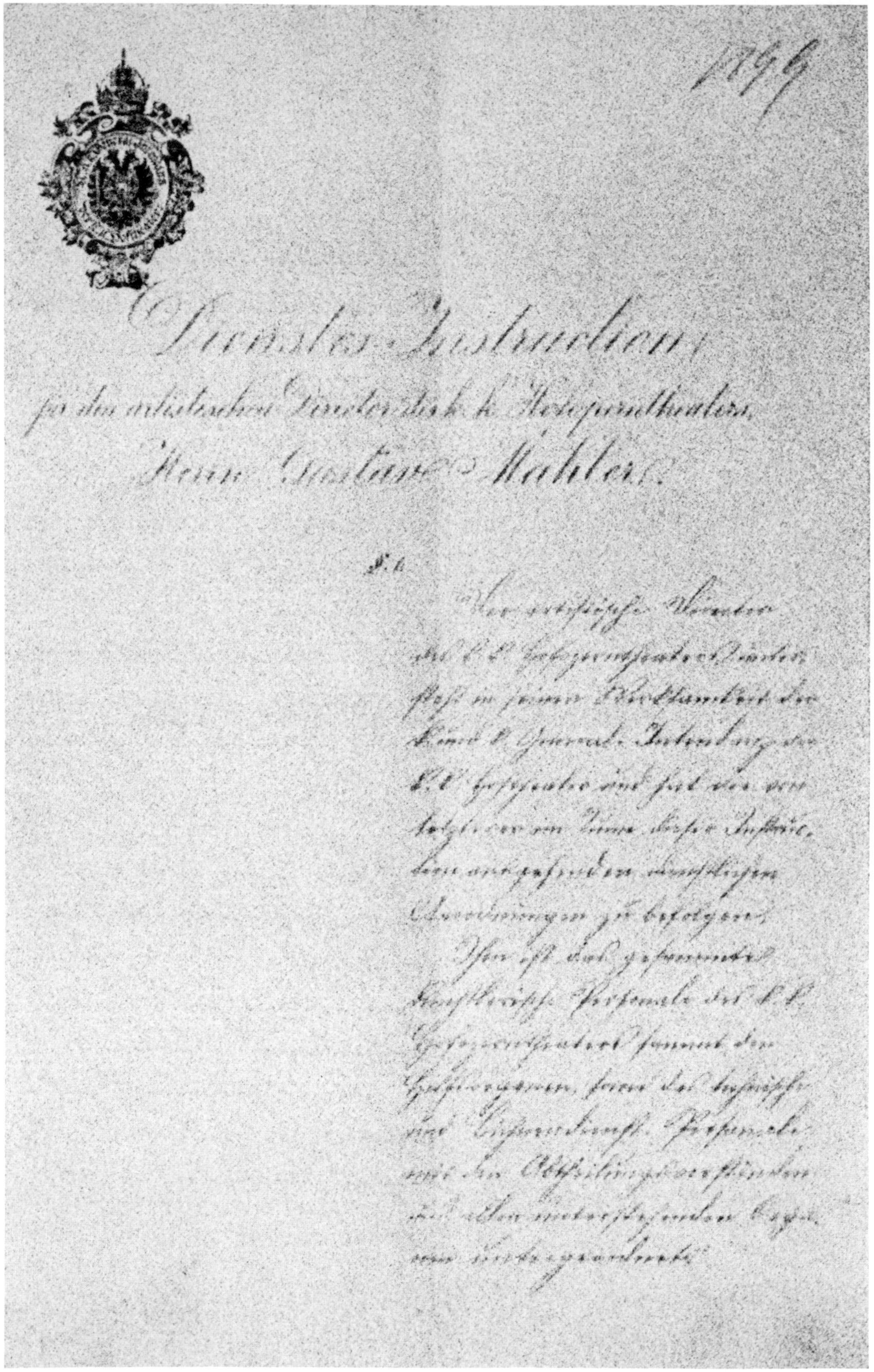

1896

Dienstes-Instruction

für den artistischen Director des k. k. Hofoperntheaters

Herrn Gustav Mahler.

§. 1.

GUSTAV MAHLER
AS DIRECTOR OF THE VIENNA OPERA

Marcel Prawy

Large opera houses have always tended to acquire an especial glory when great composers are at their head: under Carl Maria von Weber in Dresden, under Meyerbeer in Berlin, under Liszt in Weimar, under Richard Strauss in Vienna – though in connection with Vienna, Gustav Mahler should be mentioned before Strauss, not only because he directed the Vienna Opera during the decade from 1897 to 1907 but also because Mahler brought into being no more and no less than a completely new way of hearing and seeing opera, a reformatory act which he endeavoured to carry through with unbelievable energy. His fanaticism as director of the Vienna Opera was such that he only allowed himself time for his own composition during the summer holidays or in the early morning. He possessed colossal strength of purpose and sufficient inner strength to carry out whatever he wanted, so that one can only describe the Mahler decade in Vienna as probably the most important period in opera direction there has ever been.

For my parents' generation the Mahler era was *the* great experience, *the* great event. I have often heard my father recalling just how tensely the public waited for the conductor to appear before the opera actually began because in those days the name of the conductor was not yet printed on the cast list or playbill. People craned

Far left: Gustav Mahler's appointment by Rudolf Prinz von und zu Liechtenstein as Kapellmeister of the Imperial Vienna Opera.
Left: The first page of the "Instructions for the artistic director of the Imperial Opera", dating from 1899, issued by Fürst Montenuovo.

their necks from the fourth gallery, trying to be the first to recognize the maestro. And they were disappointed if they discerned a full beard (for Hans Richter, Bruno Walter and Franz Schalk had beards). It was different when the clean-shaven Mahler hurried nimbly through the orchestra pit, the extremely pale, small man, who looked like E. T. A. Hoffmann's conductor, Kreisler. Before he swung himself up on to the conductor's podium, which had been raised especially for him, it could happen that he stamped his foot or suddenly stopped in his tracks, stood still and looked as if he was – as in the lied he composed – temporarily "lost to the world". Not only did Mahler have the podium raised, he also had it pushed right up to the string players, which was an innovation. His predecessor Jahn, for instance, sat on a round cane chair in the middle of the orchestra and still earlier operatic conductors had their podiums placed right up to the ramp so that the musicians virtually sat behind them; this did not really seem to bother the maestri much since they were primarily concerned with the singers and what was happening on the stage. The position of the conductor's podium as we know it today (and which we take for granted) was first set by Felix von Weingartner, Mahler's successor.

All accounts agree that Mahler's demonic nature communicated itself to the audience and electrified it. This is why he was universally assured of admiration as a conductor even though, after ten years in office, Mahler the opera director was driven out in the most ignominious manner. At the beginning, the conductor fascinated people with his furious élan, with his impetuous beats, which reminded one of whistling slashes through the air, and later with his more tranquil mastery.

His contact with singers was magical, particularly when he liked one of them. In such cases his mode of accompanying was imploring and questioning; but when for some reason or another he flew into a rage he held his baton like a stiletto. He was merciless to the public as well; his contemporaries have recalled that he could behave like a "fascinating barbarian" if, for instance, there was applause during the orchestral postlude after an aria. His interpretation of the overture to Mozart's *Don Giovanni* is said to have been an orgiastic "brio" while his *Meistersinger* lasted longer than when Hans Richter was conducting it. His "forte" was as passionate as his "piano" was uncompromising – often a great deal calmer than the feast of sound so beloved of his contemporaries.

No less a person than Brahms, when he was in Vienna, raved about a performance of *Don Giovanni* which he had heard in Budapest, with Mahler conducting. And Rosa Papier, the Vienna Opera singer who had sung at a German musical festival under Mahler's direction, wrote to her husband, the distinguished critic Dr. Hans

78

Oberhofmeister Fürst Alfred Montenuovo, who was also senior to the Intendant of the Imperial Opera.

Previous page: The Hofburg in Vienna with the Franzensplatz and view of the Amalienburg wing. In the foreground, the monument to Emperor Franz I. Fürst Montenuovo's office was in the Hofburg.

Paumgartner, in enthusiastic terms about a conductor by the name of Gustav Mahler. Only a few of the initiated knew that he had already composed three symphonies, even though they had not yet been performed, even in Vienna. But Obersthofmeister Prince Liechtenstein listened to these "initiated" voices and took the risk of proposing that the Kaiser engage this conductor as the director of the Opera. The fact that this unconventional proposal was then indeed accepted comes close to one of those rare but nonetheless occasional "Austrian miracles". With the Emperor's approval, Baron Dr. Josef von Bezecny appointed Mahler to be director of the opera. Bezecny was general manager and at the same time, in his capacity as a financial expert, governor of the Bodenkreditanstalt and president of the *Gesellschaft der Musikfreunde*.

Mahler spent the summer of 1896 at the Attersee, devoting his time to his own creative work, while Brahms was staying nearby in Bad Ischl where Mahler visited him. One would certainly not be wrong in assuming that the talks between these two included a large project which touched on the dream of Mahler's life, namely to take over the direction of the Vienna Opera. Brahms, who died the following year, made a protégé of Mahler, the ardent Wagnerian, whereas from Bayreuth, Cosima Wagner was doing her best to prevent "Mahler the Jew" from getting the post. On 11 May 1897 he made his debut as Kapellmeister in Vienna with an enthusiastically praised performance of *Lohengrin*. His official appointment was made in October after the powers that be had, by the fait accompli, forced his ailing predecessor, Wilhelm Jahn, to step down. Mahler tried to push through the much-discussed reforms (and not only the musical ones) concerning the running of an opera-house as quickly as possible. So it was that he ordered the auditorium to be completely darkened – something which today we take for granted. He also did away with a despised institution such as the claque – the claque was rated as a "semi-official" institution for which a number of seats in the gallery were reserved every day – following excesses occurring at the première of Smetana's *Dalibor*. Mahler had this abolished and every singer had to sign a declaration stating that he would not employ a paid claque. However, the success of this step very soon left much to be desired for no singer willingly dispensed with the claque of "spontaneous applause"; they declared themselves powerless against the claque while at the same time paying them higher fees. Mahler showed himself to be merciless to latecomers to the opera (except for those occupying boxes or standing room) and they were rigorously excluded until the interval.

As already stated, Gustav Mahler was the personification of correctness, discipline and precision – he regarded these virtues as being a *conditio sine qua non* of every artistic action. He originated the expression (later often misquoted) "tradition is the same as slovenliness"; he hated inexactitude and unpunctuality and if, for instance, during a rehearsal a lazy singer promised, in the words of the saying, that "it will be all right on the night", that he would work harder and concentrate more on the evening itself, Mahler came near to "primeval rages" and was consequently much feared on this account. The whole business of rehearsal at the opera was remodelled and firmly organized. In Ferdinand Foll, Mahler had found a Studienleiter who suited him and one who enjoyed Mahler's confidence. Nevertheless, Mahler took most of the rehearsals himself. It is said that when doing this, sitting hunched over the piano, oblivious of himself and overwhelmed by visions, he played and sang as if he had already penetrated the ecstatic realms of his later symphonies.

But Mahler the fanatic did not only insist on strict discipline – he was perhaps even more fastidious concerning productions (Mahler had directed all the important new operas of his era himself). Whereas over such matters his predecessor Jahn would sit in one of the rear boxes and would establish contact with the stage by telephone, Mahler preferred to sit in the second box in the second circle from which he could at any time dash over to the stage in order to intervene (his telephone was on his conductor's podium). He demanded as much of his singers as he did of himself; he expected each of them to have complete mastery of his current part and when Wagner was being played he demanded that the singers read the writings of the composer which he (Mahler) himself admired. When someone else was producing, he used to let his mind wander for minutes at a time. Bruno Walter used to relate an anecdote about how once during a rehearsal Mahler called out "Bill, please" when a producer gave him the sign to start playing again. On the other hand, he had a sense of humour. Once, when he was in full agreement with a singer down to the last detail, he said to him: "Don't look so slavishly at the conductor or you might regret it when, in *Siegfried,* you sing to him: 'It is a horse, resting in deep sleep!'"

During the first five years, that is to say during the first half of the period when he was director, Mahler produced many of the repertory works in what was then a completely new form. The cadenzas and florid improvisatory embellishments which had crept into *Figaro,* for example, were ruthlessly cut. In *Götterdämmerung* he included the Norns scene which up till then had always been cut and reinstated many other customary cuts with the result that a Mahler performance of *Götterdämmerung* lasted more than an hour longer than under other conductors' batons. He used a revolving stage for the first time in *Cosi fan tutte* and accompanied the recitatives himself at the piano, later on the harpsichord. He replaced the romantic rendering of the gruesome Wolf's Glen in *Freischütz* by effective interplay of light

Josef von Beseczny, Hoftheaterintendant, who engaged Gustav Mahler in 1897.

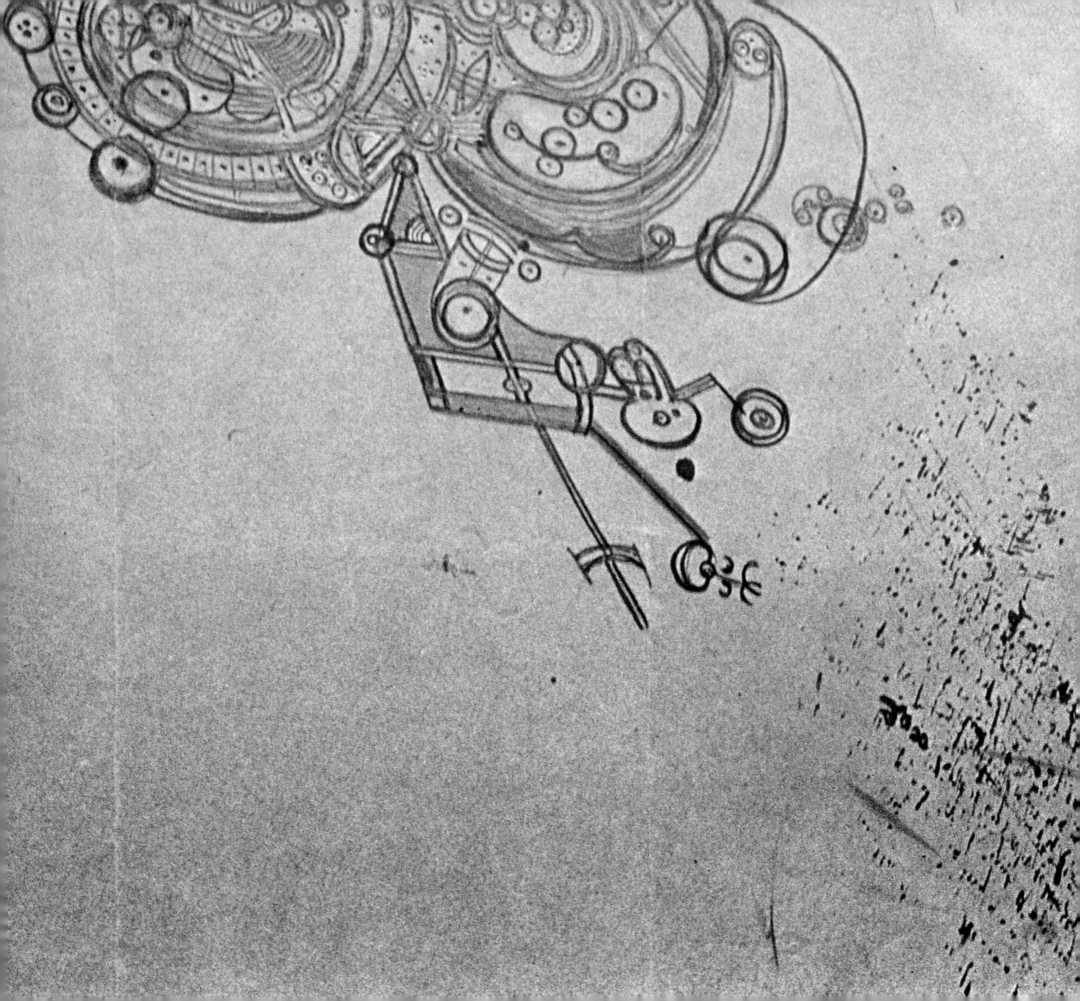

and shade effects which elicited from his opponents the remark that "the wolf's glen scene had turned into a harmless rendezvous in the Purkersdorf Wood".

His preference for Slavonic music showed itself in new productions of three of Tschaikovsky's works (*Eugene Onegin*, *Queen of Spades* and *Iolanta*), in Rubinstein's *The Demon* and Smetana's *Dalibor*. He did not in any way neglect his contemporaries; he had already produced Leoncavallo's *Bohème* one year after Alexandrine von Schonerer, the head of the Theater an der Wien, had secured Puccini's opera of the same name: Puccini's *La Bohème* was only included in the Vienna Opera repertory in 1903. In 1899 Mahler put on *Der Bärenhäuter* by Siegfried Wagner, the talented son of the Bayreuth maestro, in Vienna but it had no lasting success. The following saying was going round Vienna at the time: "The Emperor wants to ennoble Siegfried Wagner because he prefers 'Siegfried von Wagner' (Wagner's *Siegfried*) to Siegfried Wagner." In 1902, a new star appeared on the operatic horizon for the first time in Vienna: the successful première of Richard Strauss' *Feuersnot* had taken place at the Vienna Opera.

Both Mahler and Hans Richter were confirmed Wagnerians even though basically of completely differing temperaments. Yet Mahler took pains to keep the underlying conflicts in check, though on the other hand he could not conceal his different interpretation of Wagner. One day in 1900 he declared that he personally would conduct all Wagner performances. Richter thereupon left the Vienna Opera and up to the day of his death in 1918 never again conducted in Vienna. Mahler eventually found a more suitable "substitute" in the person of Franz Schalk who came from the Bruckner circle; an engagement which was only a limited blessing since Schalk was a good conductor but not one to sweep everything before him, though he worked for many years as a diligent opera director.

Bruno Walter, Mahler's friend from his Hamburg days, was engaged in Vienna, where to start with he conducted mostly the Italian and French repertory and in so doing laid the foundations for what he was one day to become: one of the foremost conductors in the world. Mahler brought an imposing collection of singers to Vienna though he declined to have typical "perfect voices". He preferred bigger, rather harder, brittle voices capable of a greater degree of expression and whose owners understood how to turn the spirit of the roles they were playing into sound and to express their own comprehension in gestures: singers like Anna von Mildenburg, subsequently the wife of Hermann Bahr. Mahler had become acquainted with this pupil of Rosa Papier's in Hamburg and had a very high regard for her – he thought she might be suitable for very dramatic roles. Indeed, Mildenburg matured very quickly

Above: Selma Kurz started her career as a mezzo-soprano. She was discovered by Gustav Mahler and under his guidance she became a coloratura soprano. The "Kurz trills" became known all over the world.
Left: During negotiations when seated at his desk, Mahler used to "scribble" with lead pencil or crayon on blotting or writing paper. By their unconscious, amusing ornaments, these "by-products" show Mahler's same typical strong feeling for shape as in his compositions.

83

Press report on the reasons behind Mahler's resignation as director of the Imperial Opera.

and became an incomparable Isolde and Brünnhilde; in addition, she was a devoted disciple of Mahler's. The newly-engaged Dane, Erik Schmedes, played opposite her as Tristan and Siegfried; Mahler is supposed to have "explained" *Tristan* to him as follows: "Before the love-potion, sing like a baritone, afterwards as a tenor."

Understandably, the élan, the tempo and the lack of compromise with which Mahler whipped through his reforms were not to the taste of all the members of the opera. For instance, Marie Renard took leave of her public amid tumultuous applause as Carmen and married a Count Kinsky, while at the same time two excellent tenors, Ernest van Dyck and Franz Naval, also left the opera house. The latter had been the first Rodolfo in Puccini's *Bohème*. They did not fit the legendary ensemble of so-called "Mahler singers" who flocked round the maestro and whose fanaticism caused people to compare them with members of an order or of a fraternity. Thereafter Mahler engaged Marie Gutheil-Schoder from Weimar to succeed Marie Renard in Vienna. At first she had a hard time getting through to the public because of her harsh voice; however, thanks to her personality, she gradually managed to become the public's darling. The bass, Friedrich Weidemann, was the new Wotan and the new Hans Sachs, and Richard Mayr, later to become very famous, was another colleague. Mahler engaged Leopold Demuth from Brünn to be the leading baritone; under Mahler's guidance, he became a famous Wolfram and Dutchman. He brought Selma Kurz from Bielitz; she was originally a mezzo-soprano but he trained her to become a coloratura prima donna. Mahler noticed at a rehearsal that Kurz liked to hold her trills rather a long time: he trained this ability and timed it systematically with a stopwatch until the "Kurz trills" acquired renown as a phenomenon in opera houses and concert halls all over the world. In the great aria in *Lucia di Lammermoor* she achieved such artistic unity with the flute that it was impossible to tell when the flute and when the voice came in. Kurz also sang Mimi under Mahler and even Butterfly.

But probably the most popular singer of all whom Mahler brought to Vienna was Leo Slezak – a giant of a man, formerly a locksmith, who came from Schönberg in Moravia. His voice, as wide-ranging as it was flexible, was just as capable of the softest pianissimos as of violent dramatic outbursts; his repertoire extended from Mozart to Meyerbeer and Wagner. He became one of the most celebrated singers in the world. Thanks to his irrepressible sense of humour (he was famous for trying to divert his partners from their entries by telling jokes) he later began a second career as a comic, especially in films, and wrote a number of humorous books.

Mahler graduated from reformer to revolutionary, especially during the second half of his reign as director, that is to say, from 1902 onwards, because, having remo-

KAIS. KÖN. HOF- OPERNTHEATER.

Definitive Eintheilung der Vorstellungen

vom *Sonntag 5. Februar* bis *Samstag 11. Februar* 1899.

Tage	Vorstellungen	Rollen-Besetzung		Anmerkung
		Damen	**Herren**	*Dirigent*
Sonntag den 5.	35. Ab. Vorstllg. *Lohengrin*			*Dir. Mahler*
Montag den 6.	36. Ab. Vorstllg. *Eugen Onegin*			*Dir. Mahler*
Dienstag den 7.	37. Ab. Vorstllg. *Die weiße Dame*			*Dir. Mahler*
Mittwoch den 8.	38. Ab. Vorstllg. *Die Puppenfee / Zeppelin*			*Dir. Mahler / Bayer*
Donnerstag den 9.	39. Ab. Vorstllg. *Afrikanerin*			
Freitag den 10.	40. Ab. Vorstllg.			*Dir. Mahler / Bayer*
Samstag den 11.	41. Ab. Vorstllg. *wie am 10.*	*do.*	*do.*	*Dir. Mahler / Bayer*
Sonntag				

In Mahler's day the name of the conductor still did not appear on the playbill. The names of the cast and conductor could only be obtained from the management schedules which appeared every week. Alterations made at short notice were entered in red ink.

delled the music and acting, he went ahead with innovating a completely new way for hearing and seeing operatic production. He began this, above all, by realizing the idea of the cycle: wholly in the sense of the Wagnerian term "Gesamtkunstwerk" he visualized first of all the production of the masterpieces in the German repertory, that is to say Gluck, Mozart and Wagner, in new musical and scenic concepts. To

Above: The wages of the directors of the Imperial Opera. As former director of the Royal Opera in Budapest Mahler was also entitled to a pension.
Right: Detail of the Vienna Opera House. Gustav Mahler's office was in this section of the building.

do this, it became clear that it was urgently necessary to renovate the stock of stage equipment completely, because what Mahler had found was stage scenery naturalistically painted which surrounded the stage area – offering room for crowd scenes and the ballet dancers – more a decorated framework than stage architecture. And having scenery designed in the spirit of the work being performed was of prime importance to him. So he had to look around for an equally ingenious partner with the same sort of ideas. Something along the lines of the book by Adolphe Appia which had just been published, *Music and Production*; Mahler was very enthusiastic about some of the ideas in it. Appia, with his demand for a stage area which was only hinted at simply by the use of colour and light, anticipated much of what in our time has become known as Wieland Wagner's "New Bayreuth". The man whom Mahler eventually selected as being his equal, Alfred Roller, was to make theatrical history. Following an exchange of ideas about the possible realization of *Tristan* using new stylistic elements, Mahler and Roller drew closer together – indeed, one can say that Mahler increasingly came under Roller's spell, so much so that he, Mahler, who was otherwise incontestably authority itself in person and accustomed to having his orders obeyed, behaved in an almost childlike, shy manner in Roller's presence. In 1903, on the twentieth anniversary of Richard Wagner's death, Mahler and Roller created a new production of *Tristan and Isolde* for the Vienna Opera which for years, if not decades, was to set a stylistic trend and thereby to show how true the motto is that today's experiment becomes tomorrow's law.

The sparseness of what was only a mere suggestion of scenery – a presentiment of the New Bayreuth trend towards "cleaning up rubbish" – was compensated for by an intoxication of colour and light. Tristan (Schmedes) and Isolde (Mildenburg) drank their magic potion in the first act amidst an absolute explosion of orange and red, and in the second act Marke's palace (the part was sung by Richard Mayr) was set against a darkening sky of violet and blue, while the third act, around the linden tree on top of the rocky crags, symbolized the sad melody of death in multifarious shades of grey. The première was a sensation; everyone wrote about Roller's "Lichtmalerei" and Mahler's "Lichtmusik" which one could "almost see with one's eyes" – at any rate they agreed that they had experienced a scenic revolution, even if many people found some parts of Roller's "light show" too dark.

At any rate Mahler was able to get Roller to sign a contract with the Vienna Opera. Their next joint venture was Beethoven's *Fidelio* which, incidentally, is everywhere today performed in the same form as at that performance: the third *Leonora Overture*, which until then had been played in the interval (Hans Richter had even put

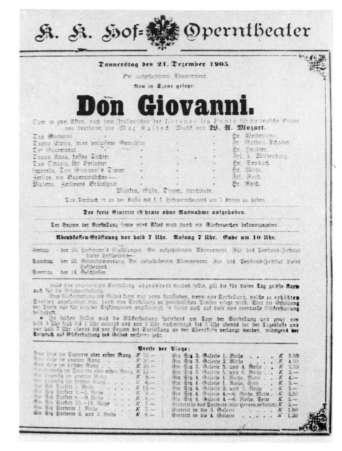

Two playbills from the Vienna Opera. The successful collaboration between Gustav Mahler and Alfred Roller began with *Tristan und Isolde*.
Left: Gustav Mahler in 1907.

it at the beginning and cut the E Major Overture), was placed where it belonged, namely between the dungeon scene and the finale; only here is it really able to reflect suffering and triumph. It was unprecedentedly realistic – the way the prisoners crept out of the gloomy holes in the wall – the way the guards appeared as menacing shadows. One curious point – Erik Schmedes had Florestan's big aria transposed a whole tone down!

Mahler and Roller commemorated Mozart's 150th birthday by organizing a Mozart cycle, beginning with *Don Giovanni*. Roller's "towers" have since become famous (throughout the opera they acted as boundaries to the stage – wide grey pillars on either side and yet from one scene to the next they assumed a different significance and function). Only the central portion of the scenery was changed; the towers, which made rapid scene changing possible, were not only the Commendatore's house and Elvira's balcony but also both interior and exterior of Don Giovanni's castle. This method was adopted later by both Schuh and Neher. Mahler allowed the Roller towers to be used for *Die Entführung aus dem Serail*, partly be-

Gustav Mahler on the conductor's podium, a silhouette by Otto Böhler.
Right: Partial view of the auditorium of the Opera which was built between 1861 and 1869 by Eduard van der Nüll and August Siccard von Siccardsburg and which opened on 25 May 1869 with a performance of *Don Juan*.

cause he was so enthusiastic about their versatility and partly for reasons of economy. Incidentally, Giovanni's descent into hell was the final scene; the concluding sextet was left out.

A new *Figaro* followed in 1906 in which, in order to make Marcellina's legal claim clearer, Mahler had the Beaumarchais original judgment scene put in for which he composed his own secco recitative and accompanied it himself on the harpsichord.

Some of the other exciting joint work done by Mahler and Roller was Wagner's *Rheingold* (1905) and *Walküre* (1907), uncut, in which Roller's fantastic cloud and light projections during the ride of the Valkyries caused a furore. In 1905 Mahler began to correspond with Richard Strauss in order to acquire the performing rights to Strauss' *Salome*. This bold venture was of course frustrated by the "local censorship authorities", as Mahler wrote – the reason being that John the Baptist was brought on to the stage, that the name of Christ was mentioned and that the whole thing was a "shocking subject" belonging in the realm of "sexual pathology", certainly not on the Imperial operatic stage. So it was that Gluck's *Iphigenia in Aulis*, with Marie Gutheil-Schoder in the title role, became the last joint Mahler-Roller première. The characters were directed in the sense of antique "reliefs", the opera was played in front of a curtain which only at the end was opened to show the harbour.

In a typical "Mahler year" the Vienna Opera repertory consisted of, on average, 54 operas and 16 ballets, among them pioneering premières of works by Mahler's own contemporaries such as Hans Pfitzner, who enjoyed a close friendship with Mahler, and the latter performed Pfitzner's opera *Die Rose vom Liebesgarten* against considerable opposition, even from the orchestra. Eugene d'Albert was also represented on the programme with two one-act operas, Wolf-Ferrari with his *Die neugierige Frauen*. New operas by Leo Blech, Nikolaus von Reznicek and Ludwig Thuille were included as well as an opera by Alexander von Zemlinsky, who actually worked for a while as conductor at the Vienna Opera. If Mahler was not content with the preparations for a première he would postpone it without giving it a thought, as in 1903, when Gustave Charpentier's *Louise* was to be played and at the last minute the composer came along with alterations he wanted in the production which Mahler thought were interesting. Or in the tragic case of Hugo Wolf, to whom Mahler had assured "free tickets for life": Wolf was already mentally deranged and first learned from Mahler of the acceptance of his opera *Der Corregidor;* but the first performance was repeatedly delayed so that Hugo Wolf died without having seen the première. The posthumous performance was no more than a perfunctory success. Mahler was all for what was new even if it was not necessarily crowned with success.

From left: Leo Slezak as Walter von Stolzing in *Die Meistersinger von Nürnberg*, Richard Mayr as Marke and Anna von Mildenburg as Isolde in *Tristan und Isolde*.
Right: The drop curtain designed by Alfred Roller in 1905 for *Don Giovanni*.

Among the few of the current new works which he let slip through his fingers were *Tosca, Tiefland* and *Pelléas and Mélisande*. Caruso came to Vienna as a guest singer in 1906 and 1907, Gemma Bellincioni, the Italian diva, created the part of Giordano's Fedora in Vienna, and when such guests were playing Mahler insisted on the whole ensemble singing in Italian. He was altogether more tolerant with guests than with the singers in his own opera house. He allowed the famous Nellie Melba, for example, to rise up after the end of *Traviata*... to sing the mad scene from *Lucia di Lammermoor*!

In Vienna Mahler had as many admirers of his sensational overall effects as he had enemies. But he never achieved "popularity" – he was too single-minded of purpose, noncommittal and "uncomfortable". It is well known that uncompromising intellectual fanaticism, precisely in Vienna, always comes up against bitter reactions because it is felt that it is "disturbing" and there was absolutely nothing Viennese about Mahler in this sense. His divided nature prevented this *a priori*. If there was anything "Viennese" about him, it was his preference for the coffeehouse. Before and after performances he frequented the "Imperial", which was well known because

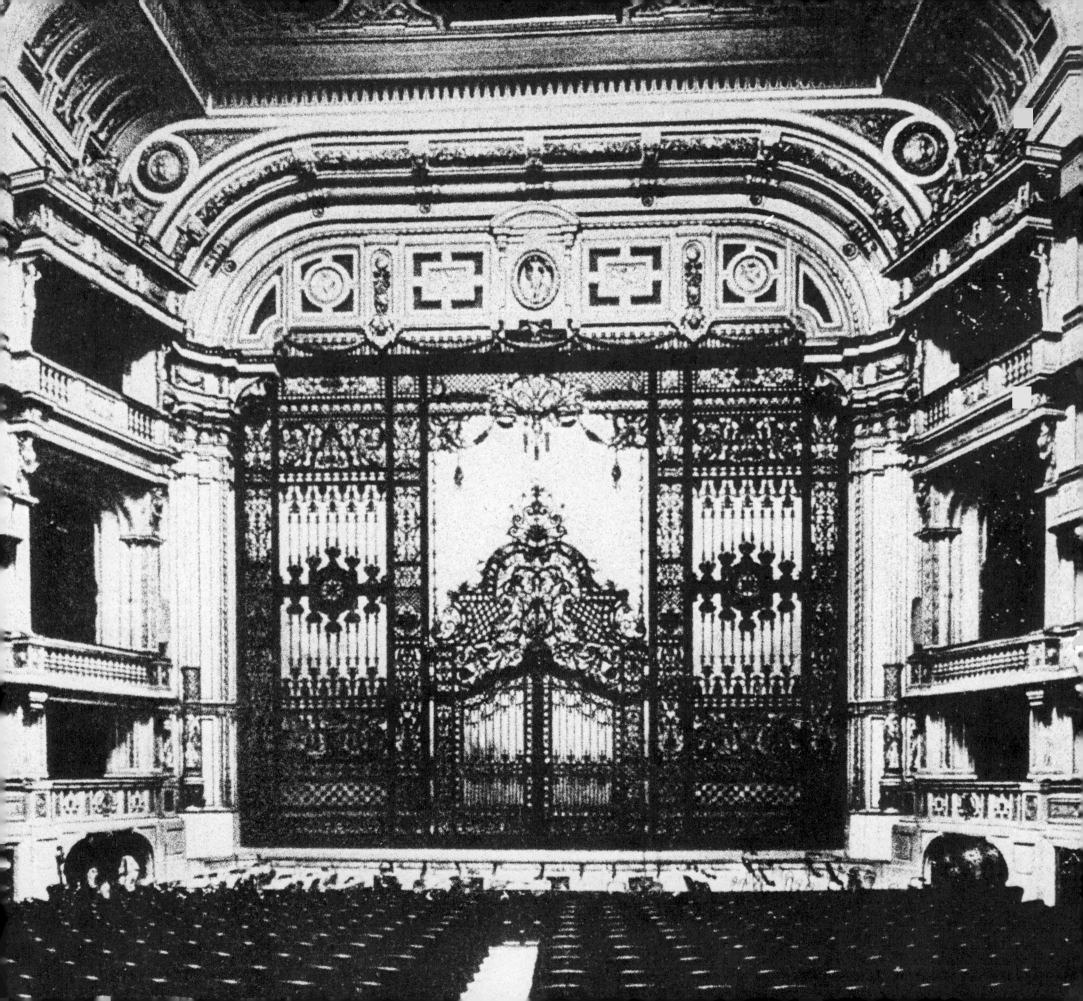

Right: Alfred Roller, who was Mahler's most important collaborator during his directorship at the Vienna Opera.
Above: Roller's signet.
Left: Alfred Roller's sketch for Act II of *Tristan und Isolde*. With this production, Gustav Mahler commemorated the 20th anniversary of the death of Richard Wagner and at the same time created a milestone in the history of the interpretation of this work.

Alfred Roller's designs for the stage sets for *Don Giovanni*.
Above: The Commendatore's garden in Act I, Scene I. Centre:
In Donna Anna's House, Act II, Scene 4. Below: The sketch
of the stage.

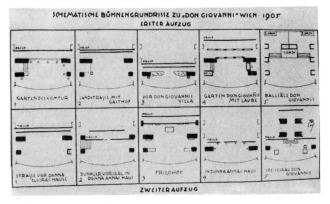

there one could possibly contrive to have things brought to the ears of the Emperor himself by means of Katherina Schratt's tarot partners. There he was jovial, whether discussing the most recent première, whether reading what the critics had to say. ("What have the superiors written?" he used to ask.) According to Max Graf, he is once supposed to have said in the coffeehouse: "In forty years no one will play Beethoven symphonies any more – mine will have taken their place."

No wonder a front was being formed against him with increasing intensity – Mahler, the sensitive man always in the centre of the crossfire of "for and against". Because of this, the last few years of his time as a director were spent in the shadow of a campaign of agitation against him coming from many sides. The Vienna Philharmonic Orchestra, with whom he was never really popular because of his unrelenting attitude, took the same line as ageing singers, or singers who felt they had been pushed into the background; a large section of the press attacked him over some of his trips abroad to get his works performed elsewhere; one found fault with the "dark Rollerism" on the Viennese opera stage; German nationalistic circles were demanding a more "German" programme; the intriguers were circulating rumours about Mahler's alleged "delusions about being Caesar"; many of his weaknesses were further hawked about in exaggerated form; in a word, the whole machinery of the Viennese cabal was obviously functioning better. "Up there", of course, one reacted against the whole campaign only when it concerned the budget; expenditure was increasing in about the same ratio as income was diminishing – an old Viennese operatic aria. Mahler, who had already threatened to resign in 1905 when the court censor thwarted the performance of *Salome* (Mahler wanted the first performance to take place at the same time as in Dresden), finally capitulated in the summer of 1907 in face of the revolt which was unleashed against him: he resigned then definitively, although the most important names in Austria, such as Schnitzler, Zweig, Freud, Klimt, Schönberg and many others, tried to make him reverse his decision in what became a historic petition. Mahler conducted at the Vienna Opera for the last time on 15 October 1907; he finally took his leave with *Fidelio*. "The time has come to write finis to our joint work. I shall take leave of the workshop I have grown to love and I bid you farewell." This was the beginning of the text of a notice "to the honourable members of the Vienna Opera" which Mahler had put up on the noticeboard. He left behind in the drawer of his desk all his honours and decorations and embarked for America to conduct the Metropolitan Opera and concerts with the New York Philharmonic Orchestra. About a hundred friends and followers, among them Schönberg and Zemlinsky, accompanied him to the Westbahnhof to say good-bye.

On the 150th anniversary of the birth of Wolfgang Amadeus Mozart, Gustav Mahler conducted and produced *Don Giovanni* with the stage designs by Alfred Roller. This was the start of the famous *Mozart-Zyklus* which continued in 1906 with *Die Hochzeit des Figaro*.
Above: Alfred Roller's sketch for the cemetery scene in Act II, Scene 3 of *Don Giovanni*.

97

Design by Alfred Roller for the dungeon scene in *Fidelio*. Gustav Mahler conducted and produced the work in October 1904.

99

Alfred Roller's sketch for the prisoners' costumes in *Fidelio*.

As the train was leaving, Mahler said to his wife: "Repertory opera is a thing of the past. I am glad that I shall not be here to share in its decline." Prophetic words which have retained their topicality. And yet Mahler did go back to Vienna, to die there. His heart complaint had worsened while he was in the New World; he returned to Vienna a sick and broken man – to that city which he had both loved and hated. In May 1911, "the rejected one", as he called himself, was laid to rest in the Grinzing cemetery on a wet and windy day but in the presence of a large number of mourners. In his farewell letter to his colleagues at the Vienna Opera he had written: "Instead of a complete great work, such as I dreamed of, I am only leaving bits and pieces – for this is in man's nature." Only now do we completely recognize the greatness of Mahler's "bits and pieces".

Gustav Mahler inside the Vienna Opera house, 1903.
In the same year Alfred Roller was appointed "head
of design".

Henry-Louis de La Grange

GUSTAV MAHLER'S PRIVATE LIFE IN VIENNA

Mahler's return to Vienna in 1897 as conductor at the Imperial Opera was the most important event in his whole life and career. He had indeed travelled a long way since that autumn day when the eager small-town boy first confronted the Austrian capital, a Jewish boy in a city where anti-Semitism was virulent among all classes of society. In fact, Mahler's Jewishness, added to the rumours about his bad temper and "tyrannical nature", meant that his nomination had to be prepared in total secrecy. His main supporter in this predicament was Rosa Papier, an ageing contralto who was now one of Vienna's best-known singing teachers. For a long time, she had been the mistress of a highly placed official in the Opera "Intendanz".

By some quirk of fate, Mahler's nomination was announced on 8 April, just two days after Brahms, who had strongly supported it, was buried. Wilhelm Jahn, the former director, was still officially in charge, but Mahler was told he could take over as soon as the old man admitted that his near blindness prevented him from fulfilling his duties. He finally did so in the early autumn, and Mahler's appointment was announced on 15 October, once it had been signed by the Kaiser.

During the next ten years, Mahler was unquestionably the uncrowned king of Viennese music. This was particularly the case between October 1898 and March

Alma Schindler; a photo taken in 1899.
Left: The "Praterpartie", an oil painting by Emil Jakob Schindler (about 1879). Gustav Mahler became acquainted with the daughter of this famous Viennese painter in 1901 and in the following year he married her.

1901, when he also conducted the Philharmonic Concerts. Despite the innumerable "affairs" which erupted month after month at the Opera, and despite bitter attacks in the press, Mahler's position was never seriously threatened, largely thanks to the Habsburg court. Prince Montenuovo, the Obersthofmeister, who was responsible for running both Court Theatres, was an unswerving admirer of Mahler's human and artistic integrity – which many saw as obstinacy.

He was confronted by his first serious difficulties, however, after 1903, when he began to conduct his own works; he was away from Vienna more and more frequently. For years, he had been refusing requests for leaves of absence from Opera members who wanted to perform elsewhere, so it was difficult to claim that his own absences were less "harmful to the institution" than theirs. His stock answer to the Obersthofmeister was that the prestige he gained by his guest appearances elsewhere

From left to right: Gustav Mahler with his sister Justine and his future brother-in-law, Arnold Rosé, in 1899; Hugo Wolf, Gustav Mahler's fellow-student at the Vienna Conservatory; Berta Zuckerkandl, wife of the famous anatomist, Emil Zuckerkandl, in whose house Mahler first met his future wife, Alma; Natalie Bauer-Lechner, Mahler's friend and confidante of many years who has drawn a portrait of Mahler, the man and the artist, in her book of reminiscences.

was reflected on the whole Opera. Nevertheless, the papers kept reporting that he was "losing interest in the Opera", and in later years he was forced to limit his trips abroad. But the court officials respected his independence no less than his sense of duty. They were quite aware that he would at any time prefer to resign his post rather than compromise artistically. He never ceased to remind them how ignorant and incompetent they were outside the administrative sphere: "I didn't know you'd ever heard Beethoven's Ninth before," he told Prince Liechtenstein when the Prince suggested that Mahler's tempi were "unusual". Mahler's main struggle was always to obtain money for new productions. Sometimes he failed, as in 1905, when *Die Walküre* was planned to follow *Das Rheingold* immediately. The lack of funds meant that the production had to be postponed for two years.

Mahler's first and toughest battle with bureaucracy occurred in 1899, eighteen months after his appointment. Eduard von Wlassack, who had been so helpful to him, began to resent Mahler's "ingratitude" when he realized that he was ignoring his numerous suggestions. When the new Intendant, Freiherr August von Plappart, took up his post in February 1898, he joined Wlassack in pointing out to Prince Montenuovo in a long letter that Mahler was "reckless" when it came to money.

Plappart and Wlassack drew up a new *Dienst-Instruktion* (handbook of Opera regulations) severely curtailing the director's powers. He would be obliged, for instance, to obtain the Intendant's written consent before making any important decision, even a last-minute cast or costume change. After a glance at the new *Dienst-Instruktion*, Mahler wrote directly to the Obersthofmeister to explain that he had to

Before her marriage, Alma Schindler studied composition with Alexander Zemlinsky. Mahler forbade her to do any composing but later on, in 1910, he initiated the publication of some of her work.

have a free hand in such last-minute decisions. He drew up a list of all the unnecessary harassments he had suffered at the hands of the Intendant. It was hard enough, he explained, to run such a large theatre as the Opera, without having to cope with the Intendant's insidious resistance at every turn. Didn't Freiherr von Plappart encourage the Opera members to complain to him whenever they thought they'd been ill-treated by the Director?

If Mahler had not won this particular battle, his position at the Opera would have quickly become intolerable. But the Obersthofmeister was convinced that he was the right man in the right place and therefore sided with him against the Intendant. Every time a new "affair" broke out – a conflict with a singer or a chorus or orchestra member – and whenever Prince Montenuovo warned him not to "play into the hands of his enemies", Mahler would reply that such storms were indispensable for enforcing discipline: "Every scandal has a decided meaning and a definite effect. You should call me in to see you whenever there are fewer than two a week!"

Not all the singers, of course, sided against Mahler or challenged his authority. When he arrived at the Opera, he found a constellation of stars, the darlings of the Viennese public: Marie Renard and Ernest van Dyck, for instance, who specialized in French and Italian works and whose chief aim was to please their fans rather than to serve the music and the drama. They soon realized that life under the new director was going to be too uncomfortable and they consequently left Vienna. Hermann Winkelmann, the famous Wagnerian tenor, was an artist of higher stature, but he didn't like having his routine disturbed either. He stayed on at the Hofoper until the end of his career, frequently complaining about the new director's "tyrannical" nature. Theodor Reichmann, the Amfortas in the first Bayreuth production of *Parsifal,* and one of the greatest Wagnerian baritones in history, completely changed his mind about Mahler. At first he would call him in private a merciless despot, a "little goblin", a "Jewish monkey". But later, when Mahler forced him to reconsider his entire conception of the role of Hans Sachs for a new production and he met with greater success than ever, Mahler became "a God to be worshipped", a man who must be "forgiven everything". Other singers, like Frances Saville, Edyth Walker and Luise von Ehrenstein, fell from grace and were persuaded to resign. During the second half of Mahler's tenure, the Opera ensemble, as he created it, consisted mainly of artists such as Anna von Mildenburg, Marie Gutheil-Schoder, Erik Schmedes, Friedrich Weidemann, Willy Hesch and Richard Mayr. Besides these loyal and conscientious singers who respected and understood him well enough to tolerate an occasional fit of temper, Mahler also engaged three bel canto specialists, Selma Kurz,

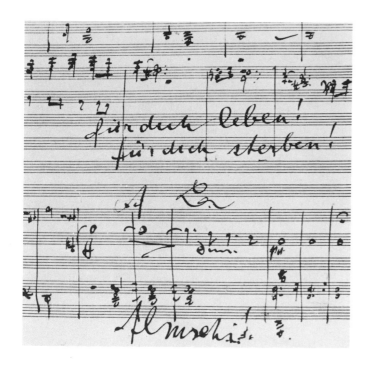

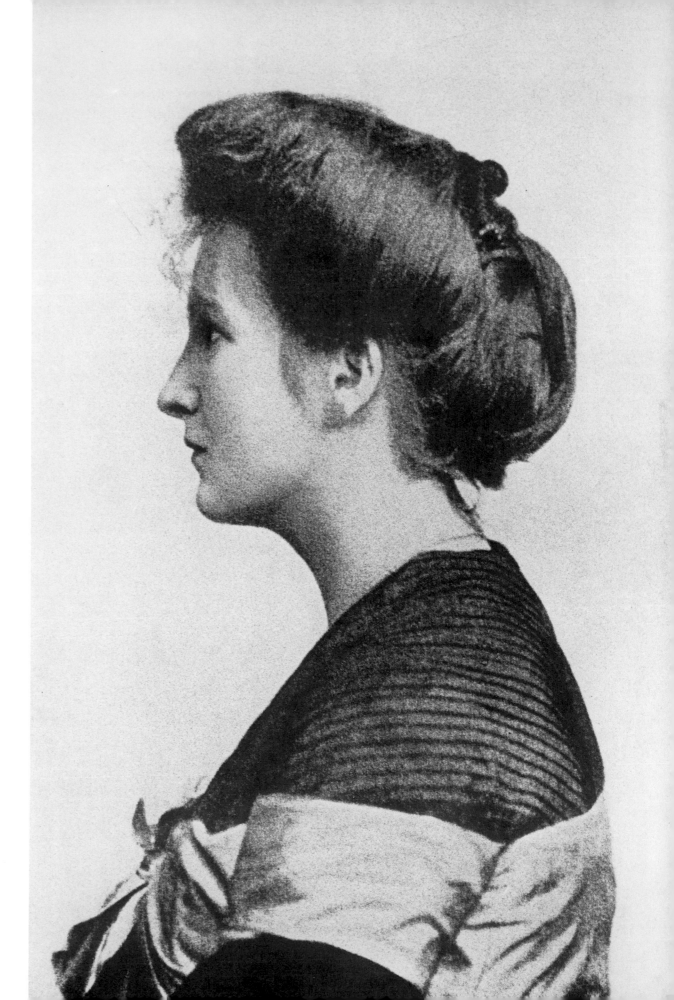

Detail from the sketches for the *Tenth Symphony*. The pet name *Almschi* refers to Alma.
Right: Alma Mahler in 1902.

Leo Slezak and Leopold Demuth, with whom he seldom saw eye to eye. For him, they were always essentially singers who were uninterested in dramatic or musical meaning. All three achieved stardom, however, and had frequent reason to complain about Mahler's rudeness. They claimed they were always brusquely rebuked whenever they wanted leave of absence, and blamed him for "taking no interest in their artistic development".

In Hamburg, Mahler's affair with Mildenburg had very nearly ended in a public scandal and ruined his career. In Vienna, he knew that he had to be careful, yet a great many rumours circulated about his love-life. Only two were probably founded on fact. His love-letters to Selma Kurz, shortly after she became a member of the Opera, show that he was indeed madly in love with her early in 1900. A few months later, the passionate admiration he expressed for Gutheil-Schoder as an artist seems to imply that he was, as people whispered, in love with her, at least for a time.

In later life and probably as a result of the intrigue, malice and hatred he had encountered, particularly at the Opera, Mahler was sometimes too easily persuaded that people disliked him. Arnold Rosé, his brother-in-law, for instance, jeopardized his relationship with the Philharmonic musicians (who played in the Opera orchestra) by repeating the disparaging remarks they made about Mahler. Yet, whenever a conflict occurred involving Rosé, Mahler would always take his side. He was also accused of invariably standing up for Alfred Roller, the great scenic designer he engaged in 1903. In 1907, for instance, when Roller organized a ballet rehearsal in his office without so much as informing Hassreiter, the ballet master, Mahler took Roller's side, though he knew his friend was definitely in the wrong. "In all the years we've been working together," Prince Montenuovo declared, "this is the first time I've seen you cover up an administrative irregularity."

Mahler's day-to-day routine hardly ever varied during his years in Vienna. Always an early riser, he sat down to his desk around seven in the morning and had his breakfast brought to him there. He always arrived at the Opera at about nine and stayed there until one. As soon as the morning's business was out of the way, he would call home to make sure lunch was ready as soon as he returned. He rang the downstairs bell of the apartment house (still standing on the corner of Rennweg and Auenbruggergasse) to warn the servants to have the soup on the table by the time he raced up four flights of stairs, hurried through the flat, slamming doors behind him, to wash his hands and dash into the dining-room.

After lunch, he generally took a short nap and then strolled with his sister Justi (or later with Alma), either in the Belvedere Park, or along the whole length of the

Ring. At five o'clock, he had tea before returning to the Opera. Even when he wasn't conducting, he was always there for at least part of every performance. He nearly always dined late at the end of the day's work. From 1897 until the end of 1901, his professional life was so full that he made virtually no new friends, though he remained faithful to those of his youth. He was certainly attached to Natalie Bauer-Lechner, his confidante and passionate admirer (whose *Mahleriana* contain so much valuable information on the early years at the Opera), though he sometimes resented her fussy, motherly and protective advice. With Justi, Natalie formed the heart of his intimate circle, which also included Albert and Nina Spiegler; Siegfried and Clementine Lipiner (Albert Spiegler's sister); Fritz and Uda Löhr; Guido Adler, the famous musicologist, who came from Mahler's hometown, Iglau; Arnold Rosé; Anna von Mildenburg; the invalid Henriette Mankiewicz, a painter and embroiderer; and Bruno Walter, whom Mahler engaged for the Opera in 1901. In her memoirs, the flamboyant Alma expresses her utter contempt for these early friends of her husband. It has to be admitted that they regarded her with suspicion. She in turn considered them second-rate, provincial and "petit bourgeois". Yet, except for Natalie, Mahler never broke with any of them, even after his marriage, in 1902, and his entry into the Moll-Secession circle opened up a variety of interesting new friendships and acquaintances. In Natalie's case, the break was unavoidable: primarily because Alma resented any woman who had been close to him, and secondly because Natalie had broken an unspoken agreement with Mahler by confessing her love and daring to hope he would one day marry her.

The Karlskirche was built between 1716 and 1739 by Johann Bernhard and Joseph Emanuel Fischer von Erlach. It is the most important sacred Baroque building in Vienna.

Although personal contacts and social ritual were probably more essential in Vienna than anywhere else for a successful professional life, and although the capital's "salons" then wielded considerable influence over the life of the city, Mahler could never be persuaded to frequent Viennese drawing rooms. The only exception was probably the salon of Countess Mysa Wydenbruck-Esterhazy of whom Mahler was genuinely fond because of her kindness, charm and intelligence. (Dr. Emil Zuckerkandl, a physician who belonged to Vienna's cultivated Jewish society, and his wife Berta, an art critic who played hostess to the local art world and visitors from abroad, also joined Mahler's intimates in later years.) Later on, Mahler was, so to speak, adopted by a number of old friends of the Molls, by Hugo and Ilse Conrat, for instance, a rich bourgeois couple in whose salon Brahms had been a regular visitor; by Fritz Redlich, a sugar manufacturer and art collector in whose country house at Göding Mahler stayed several times with Alma and the Molls; by Theobald Pollak, an old friend of Alma's parents who worked for the Ministry of Transport. Pollak's devotion to Mahler always touched him deeply; it was he who, in 1907, sent the composer a copy of Bethge's new book of Oriental poems, *Die Chinesische Flöte*, from which the texts of *Das Lied von der Erde* are drawn.

Sometimes Mahler and Alma would accept an invitation from someone in Vienna's "second" society (people like the financier Wetzl) or someone in the nobility (like the Prince von Thurn und Taxis). Such sorties invariably ended in failure. Mahler would always arrive late from the Opera, yet he would leave the table in the middle of dinner if he was bored and settle in the next room to read. According to Alma, he always made people uneasy, largely because he was incapable of small talk. Through Max Burckhard, an old friend of Alma's youth, Mahler met Gerhart Hauptmann, who became a close, if not intimate, friend. The respect and admiration which fill the playwright's letters testify to the extraordinary effect which Mahler's intelligence, sincerity and integrity had on those who could understand him. Alma's mother and stepfather became his true family in later years. He was as devoted to them as they were to him. Alfred Roller, Mahler's closest collaborator at the Opera for five years, also became a close and cherished friend. Both men shared the same attitude towards art, the same high professional aims, the same deep devotion to the "masters" and their works.

Among Vienna's musicians, his closest friends were of course his brother-in-law Arnold Rosé, and Bruno Walter, his assistant at the Opera but also a confidant and devoted admirer. Mahler always played his works to Walter while the ink was still fresh. Mahler's relationship to Richard Strauss is a long story. They met frequently

Gustav Mahler followed Arnold Schönberg's development with great interest; Mahler did not always understand him but he recognised his worth early on. For his part, Schönberg was keenly interested in promoting Mahler's work.

Gustav Mahler was a close friend of his older "colleague" Anton Bruckner. During his student days he made a piano reduction of Bruckner's *Third Symphony*: when he became a conductor he performed Bruckner's works whenever he could.

and always remained in close touch, Mahler conducting Strauss' works on several occasions in Vienna, and Strauss arranging for the premières of several of Mahler's symphonies. Their approaches to all human and artistic matters were fundamentally different, to such an extent that they never became friends in the usual meaning of the word. Mahler could never really sympathize with Pfitzner's ultra-conservative and German nationalistic views, yet he respected him as a composer, and a kind of friendship developed mainly because of the care and love Mahler lavished on the production of *Die Rose vom Liebesgarten.* The situation was reversed with Oskar Fried and Willem Mengelberg; Mahler was devoted to them because of their affectionate concern for the performance of *his* symphonies.

Yet none of these last-named musicians lived in Vienna, and Mahler saw them only occasionally. In the capital itself, his unique and unfailing instinct and, even rarer, his lack of musical prejudice allowed him to discover the true importance of Arnold Schönberg, the only real genius of the younger generation. From 1904 until the end of his life, Schönberg, his brother-in-law Zemlinsky, and their pupils played an essential part in Mahler's life. His affection for these fabulously gifted young composers was in every way reciprocated. Berg's letters and Webern's diary bear witness to the tremendous impact which Mahler's music and personality had on them at this crucial stage in their formative years.

It was Schönberg who, after persuading Mahler to become the honorary president of the "Association of Creative Artists" in 1904, organized the first performance of his orchestra lieder, including the *Kindertotenlieder.* With the *Third Symphony,* performed a month previously, this was the first genuine success Mahler met with as a composer in his adopted city. It was probably Schönberg who urged him to complete the *Kindertotenlieder,* for he obiously wanted some new Mahler songs for his Society concert in January 1905. Mahler's discovery of Schönberg dates from 1902, when he heard *Verklärte Nacht* played by the augmented Rosé Quartet. According to the Vienna papers, he considered conducting the première of Schoenberg's *Pelleas und Melisande* that January. It is well known that he attended the Viennese premières of Schönberg's *First Quartet* and *Chamber Symphony,* in 1907, and was deeply impressed. The boos and catcalls of the outraged audience infuriated him so much that he shouted back and created a public scandal of his own. On his deathbed, one of his last questions was: "Who'll take care of Schönberg now?" He certainly knew that Vienna, the most conservative of musical capitals, was the last place in the world where a young revolutionary could "take care" of himself, even after his genius had been universally recognized.

Otto Klemperer's career began with a recommendation from Gustav Mahler. They met in 1907 in Prague. Klemperer subsequently became one of the great interpreters of Mahler's music.

Yet, regardless of what Mahler, like Schönberg, had suffered at the hands of the Viennese, he never disowned his adopted city. "Homesickness has plagued me the whole time," he wrote from America to Countess Wydenbruck in 1908. "Unfortunately, contrary to my wife, who would like to stay here forever, I am a confirmed Viennese. My homesickness becomes a kind of feverish longing…" Nevertheless, two years earlier he had left Vienna for the New World with little or no regret. He had never tired either of its beauty, charm, vitality or of its music and legendary "musicality". But the Opera, with its intrigues and "affairs", and the Viennese, with their pettiness, perfidy, artistic conservatism and anti-Semitism, had indeed exhausted him. He turned his back on them forever. Forever? Newspaper reports and Opera archives suggest that he would probably have agreed to return in 1910, after Weingartner's failure, if he hadn't accepted the post of musical director of the New York Philharmonic for several years. But it was too early to give up this brilliant and exceptionally remunerative position. Later, he would very likely have relented – had he lived a few years longer.

Mahler's farewell to Vienna in 1907 was calm and dignified. The Opera authorities had refused to allow for a formal farewell performance, yet the applause was particularly ecstatic on the evening of 15 October, after his last opera: *Fidelio*. A month later, on 24 November, the real leave-taking took place at the *Musikvereinsaal* with the Philharmonic Orchestra and four soloists instead of two. This time the applause was delirious, a moving demonstration of love and respect.

For his departure, on the morning of 9 December 1907, a letter had summoned all Mahler's admirers and friends, all those who were aware of what Vienna was losing, to gather at the station. About two hundred people showed up at the Westbahnhof platform before Mahler arrived. Schönberg and Zemlinsky were there with a few pupils, Berg and Webern among them; the Molls; Justi and Arnold; several Philharmonic players; a few members of the Opera, including Marie Gutheil-Schoder and Erik Schmedes; and some painters from the now defunct Secession, including Alfred Roller and Gustav Klimt. Mahler was so surprised to see the huge crowd that he was hardly able to speak. Everyone rushed forward to shake hands and smother him in flowers. As the train started moving, he was still leaning out the window, hatless and smiling. Tears filled his eyes as he watched the crowd of friends gradually fade into the distance. Back on the platform, it was Gustav Klimt who gave voice to the thought running through everyone's mind: "Vorbei!" ("It is over!")

From then on Mahler spent very little time in Vienna on the way to and from Toblach, where he now spent his summers. In 1909, he and Alma decided to abandon

Gustav Mahler with Bruno Walter in Prague where the first performance of the *Seventh Symphony* took place in 1907.

the Auenbruggergasse apartment and stayed with the Molls, on the Hohe Warte, on the corner of the Wollergasse and the Steinfeldgasse. Mahler never again conducted in the capital: this was one of the conditions attached to his receiving an Opera pension. His only musical activity there was to rehearse some of the soloists in 1910, before the Munich première of the *Eighth Symphony*.

The story of Mahler's last visit to Vienna as a desperately sick man, in May 1911, is contained in Alma's memoirs. In Paris, the idea of seeing Vienna again had seemed to revive him, but the trip itself, on the Orient-Express, was painful. In Germany and Austria, reporters invaded the train at every station, and from then on until he died, bulletins on his health appeared in the papers at regular intervals.

On 9 May, late in the afternoon, the train pulled into Vienna. His sleeping car was taken to an empty platform which was forbidden to the public. Since the corridor was too narrow for a stretcher, Mahler had to be lifted from the train by two ambulance attendants. He bore it all with angelic patience, but his face looked worn and terribly pale. His deep-set eyes peered sadly, seeming to plead for a quick end to all this. At the Sanatorium Loew, in the Mariannengasse, flowers from friends and acquaintances spilled out of his room into the corridor. Get-well letters and telegrams arrived constantly, but his temperature kept climbing and his pulse quickening. It was obvious that the happiness of a return to Vienna hadn't interrupted the course of his dreadful illness, which was now reaching its final stages.

At 10.30 on the evening of 18 May, a furious thunderstorm broke out over Vienna. Rain streamed down, thunder reverberated through the Vienna Woods, and lightning illuminated the flooded streets as Mahler's breathing began gradually to subside. It was 11.05 p.m. when it stopped completely.

On 22 May, in the late afternoon, a brief funeral service was held in the central chapel of the Grinzing cemetery. As the hearse started climbing up towards the bare, open grave, the sky, grey and lustreless until then, opened up and the sun shone on the long burial procession. Everybody of consequence in Vienna was there, delegations from the newspapers, the Opera, the Philharmonic, the Conservatory, the Secession, a huge crowd of unknown or unfamiliar faces besides the family and friends. Did anyone there remember what Mahler had said seventeen years earlier, when Bülow's death in Hamburg gave rise to noisy demonstrations of grief? Bülow, he noted, would undoubtedly have preferred to be better treated during his lifetime, than to be so ostentatiously bewailed after death!

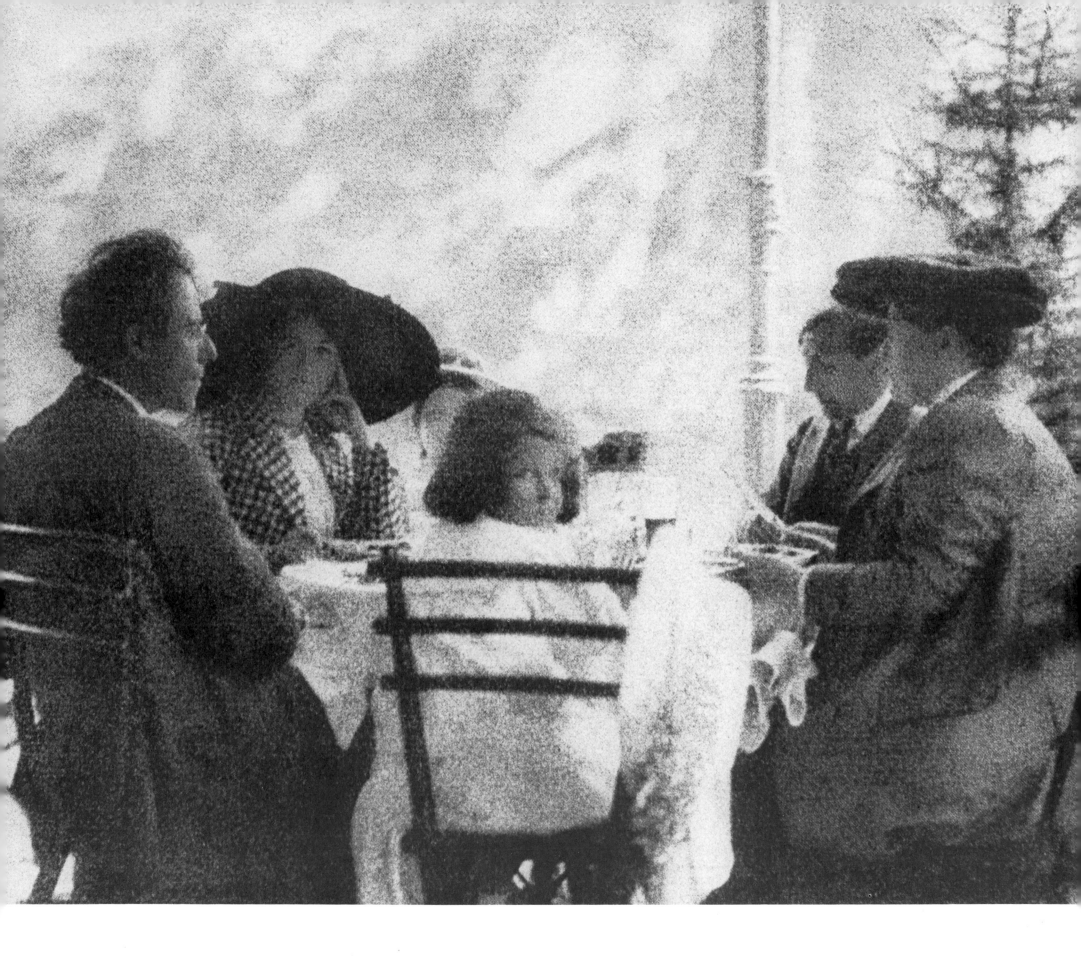

The entrance to the *Musikverein* building – an illustration from about the turn of the century. Gustav Mahler conducted the "Philharmonic" in the "Goldene Saal" in this house from 1899 to 1901.

Sigrid Wiesmann

GUSTAV MAHLER
AND THE VIENNA PHILHARMONIC ORCHESTRA

The Vienna Philharmonic Orchestra consists of members of the Opera House Orchestra – something which is a truly unique fact. In the Vienna Opera House they are subordinate to the management, while as a concert orchestra they are an independent democratic body with their own laws and they select their own conductor. The Orchestra has been in existence since 1842 when Otto Nicolai conducted the first concert in the Redoutensaal on 28 March and since 1870 regular concerts have been given in the concert hall of the *Gesellschaft der Musikfreunde,* the *Musikverein* as it is generally called.

In September 1898 a delegation from the Orchestra went to see Mahler to request him to take over the direction of the Philharmonic concerts. Mahler accepted. Hans Richter, who had conducted the Orchestra for 23 years, had resigned; the change of management in the Vienna Opera had inevitably meant restrictions in his sphere of work and, in addition, England had offered him a highly paid position. As members of the Vienna Opera Orchestra, the players had then known Mahler for a year. But the collaboration with the Vienna Philharmonic lasted barely three years, because Mahler, who was a fanatic about rehearsals, did not get on at all well with the traditional attitude of the orchestra which was one of spontaneous music-making.

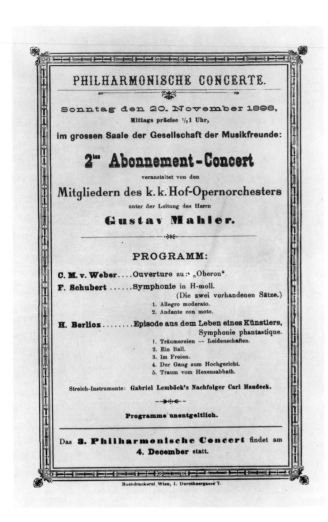

PHILHARMONISCHE CONCERTE.

Sonntag den 20. November 1898,
Mittags präcise ½1 Uhr,

im grossen Saale der Gesellschaft der Musikfreunde:

2tes Abonnement-Concert

veranstaltet von den

Mitgliedern des k. k. Hof-Opernorchesters

unter der Leitung des Herrn

Gustav Mahler.

PROGRAMM:

C. M. v. Weber.....Ouverture zu: „Oberon".
F. Schubert ....Symphonie in H-moll.
(Die zwei vorhandenen Sätze.)
1. Allegro moderato.
2. Andante con moto.
H. Berlioz.........Episode aus dem Leben eines Künstlers,
Symphonie phantastique.
1. Träumereien — Leidenschaften.
2. Ein Ball.
3. Im Freien.
4. Der Gang zum Hochgericht.
5. Traum vom Hexensabbath.

Streich-Instrumente: Gabriel Lemböck's Nachfolger Carl Haudeck.

Programme unentgeltlich.

Das 3. Philharmonische Concert findet am
4. December statt.

Buchdruckerei Wien, I. Dorotheergasse 7.

Programme leaflet of the second concert Gustav Mahler gave
with the Vienna Philharmonic Orchestra.

"He could not understand that this orchestra could only give of its best if it were given free rein. He wanted to force his will upon it completely; the orchestra was supposed to surrender its personality and its freedom of movement to his own inexorable artistic will. In this respect Mahler failed to appreciate much that was valuable but the orchestra, too, misunderstood much that was of value in Mahler." (Max Graf). At the first concert rehearsal, Josef Helmsky, the horn player, in his welcoming address stressed the fact that unfortunately the orchestra was not able to keep Hans Richter. Mahler replied: "First I must express my regret at losing a colleague as valuable as Hans Richter. Now that I find myself at the head of your admirable association, I would like to express the joy I feel at the idea of making music with you outside the theatre."

The Philharmonic Concerts, as the Sunday Matinées are called, took place about once a month. They brought together in the *Musikverein*, as they still do today, the *haute volée* in Vienna with the best orchestra.

On 6 November 1898 Mahler stood for the first time on the Vienna Philharmonic Orchestra podium (in the *Goldener Saal*). He conducted Beethoven's *Coriolanus Overture*, Mozart's *G Minor Symphony* and the *Eroica Symphony*, the work with which a few months previously Richter had concluded his period as conductor of the Vienna Philharmonic Orchestra. Mahler wanted to demonstrate that he intended to maintain the continuity of the programme but that there would be a new concept in interpretation. The concert audience also had something to learn: in the Opera House he made latecomers wait outside locked doors, while in the concert hall he prevented people from leaving the hall during a performance.

Mahler also rigorously put a stop to the prevailing custom of applauding after every movement – a wave of his hand was sufficient to make any sort of noisy interruption after the scherzo in the *Eroica* impossible. The response unmistakably showed the intensity of the effect he achieved. Whether people were enthusiastic, critical or reserved, Mahler never allowed anyone to feel indifferent. "The effect of the *Coriolanus Overture* and the *Eroica* defies description," wrote Eduard Hanslick, who admitted that he had hardly ever heard all the finest details in a piece of music sound so clear and vivid, with a total effect so overwhelmingly big and powerful. In his book about Mahler, Bruno Walter relates the story of a well-meaning friend who questioned the interpretation and Mahler replied: "Your Beethoven is not my Beethoven."

In the years to come, the problem of Beethoven enthralled him to an ever greater extent. At the fifth concert on 15 January 1899, he had the *Quartet in F Minor*, Opus

91, played by all the orchestral strings. This experiment strengthened the anti-Mahler party. Mahler, of course, knew that chamber music was intended to be played in small rooms and indeed "once chamber music is transferred to the concert hall, its intimacy is lost; but more still is lost, in a large space the four voices are weakened and do not reach the listener with the strength and intensity intended by the composer. I give them this strength by reinforcing each voice. Don't we do the same in the orchestral movements of Haydn and in the Mozart overtures? Does this alter the character of the works? Certainly not. The sound volume of a work must be adapted to the dimensions of the hall in which it is to be given…"

With Mahler it was more a question of a new and concrete way of clarifying a work. "Retouching" symphonies, not only Beethoven's, is perfectly understandable – one only has to think about the large concert halls built during the second half of the 19th century, one of which was the *Musikverein*. The volume of sound of the classical symphony was no longer sufficient. Mahler did not want a composition change – rather, he justified the alterations he made quite convincingly. There was a scandal at the Nicolai Concert on 18 February 1900 over Beethoven's *Ninth Symphony*, when he doubled the number of woodwind instruments and augmented the brass instruments by adding horns and trumpets. At the repeat performance on 22 February Mahler had an explanatory text distributed in which he quoted Wagner who had fought in word and deed for such reforms. They are not re-instrumentations, rather, as Bruno Walter put it, the results of penetrating insight into all the depths of the work and in no way a search for originality or the desire for a new subjective interpretation. Mahler lost some of the sympathy of the critics who thought highly of him as composer and opera director, and that of the Vienna Philharmonic Orchestra as well, when he prepared additional work for them by revising some of the scores. After the third subscription concert of the 1898/1899 season, Mahler conducted either first Vienna performances or a world première at almost every concert. He conducted Dvorak's *Heldenlied*, *Die Waldtaube* and the *Serenade for Wood Instruments*, Tchaikovsky's *1812 Overture* and *Manfred Symphony*, the *Roma Suite* by Bizet, Franz Liszt's *Festklänge*, Strauss' *Aus Italien* and in particular, Bruckner's *Fifth* and *Sixth Symphonies*.

Mayor Lueger invited Felix Mottl to conduct a special Philharmonic concert on 1 February 1899. This was an affront to Mahler. Indeed, the Vienna Philharmonic Orchestra, despite all the difficulties, had such a high opinion of Mahler that they inserted a new clause into their regulations according to which the Orchestra could only be conducted by its titular chief.

PHILHARMONISCHE CONCERTE.

Freitag, den 25. Jänner 1901
nachmittags 3 Uhr
im grossen Saale der Gesellschaft der Musikfreunde
General-Probe
zum
CONCERT
zu Gunsten des Vereines »NIKOLAI«, Krankencassa der Mitglieder des k. k. Hof-Opernorchesters
veranstaltet von den
PHILHARMONIKERN
unter Leitung des Herrn
GUSTAV MAHLER
k. u. k. Hofopern-Director,
sowie unter gefälliger Mitwirkung der Damen: Frau **Elise Elizza** und Frau **Laura Rado-Hilgermann**, k. k. Hof-Opernsängerinnen, der Herren: **Hermann Winkelmann**, k. u. k. Kammer- und k. k. Hof-Kapellensänger etc., **Wilhelm Hesch**, k. k. Hof-Opernsänger, der **Wiener Sing-Akademie** und des M.-G.-V. „Schubertbund".

PROGRAMM:
L. v. BEETHOVEN: Neunte Symphonie, D-moll, op. 125.

Das VI. Abonnement-Concert findet am 24. Februar 1901 statt.

Programme leaflet for the final rehearsal of Beethoven's Choral Symphony. There was a scandal at the concert itself because Gustav Mahler doubled the woodwinds and augmented the brass by adding horns and trumpets.

The "Goldene Saal" in the *Musikverein*. The *Musikverein* was built as a concert hall, conservatory and meeting house by Theophil Hansen between 1867 and 1870. It is the regular home of the Vienna Philharmonic Orchestra.

Programme leaflet of Gustav Mahler's last concert before his departure for America.

Up until 1899, Mahler "with a modesty bordering on self-deprecation kept his own composition hidden from Vienna" (Hanslick).

On 9 April 1899 he conducted one of his own symphonies for the first time: the *Second Symphony*. It was a complete success with the public; there was loud applause after every movement, though after the Scherzo there was at first a deathly silence – the audience being aware of the terrifying humour – then loud applause followed by the *Urlicht* sung by Marcella Pregi, which had to be encored. Lotte von Barenfels sang the soprano part and the choir was the *Singverein der Gesellschaft der Musikfreunde*. At the end there were lengthy ovations but Mahler was greatly disappointed by the bitter criticisms in the press.

On 18 November 1900 he conducted his *First Symphony*; there was an uproar even before the concert started because the police had refused admission to some young people who were waiting for standing room tickets. There have always been "cliques" in Vienna – for and against.

Derisive laughter greeted the Funeral March and this was drowned out by hissing; it was only the absence of a pause that prevented the majority of the audience from leaving the hall. After the last movement there was silence for a few seconds, then the first timid "Bravo" could be heard and also the counter-demonstration. The reviews were even worse than those written about his *Second Symphony*. Hanslick writes: "One of us must be mad and it isn't I!"

Hirschfeld thought that Mahler's orchestration was a "parody", others wrote of the "cacophony" of the finale.

Previously, on 14 January 1900, following Schumann's *Fourth Symphony*, the first performances in Vienna of the *Wunderhorn Lieder* with Selma Kurz singing and the last song from the *Lieder eines fahrenden Gesellen* took place successfully. Hanslick said at the time: "Now, at the beginning of a new century, it is the right moment to repeat each time to the new members of the musical Secession (Mahler, Richard Strauss, Hugo Wolf, etc.): It is very likely that the future belongs to you."

In June 1900 the Vienna Philharmonic Orchestra was invited to the International Exposition in Paris. Mahler did not want to travel because it was during his holiday period – the only time he could keep free for composition. Apart from this, he was afraid that at that time of the year the Parisian public would not be there and indeed this proved to be correct. The financial resources made available from a "guarantee fund" were quickly used up. Three concerts took place in the Théâtre Châtelet and two with the *Männergesangsverein* in the Trocadero Palace. The reviews were excellent. "We would like to express our regret that Herr Mahler, one of the most dis-

A caricature of Mahler in the *Fliegende Blätter* (Vol. 3, 1901) by Hans Schliessmann. At that time there were people who found Mahler's style of conducting particularly shocking.

tinguished symphony composers of the German school, did not include one of his own works in the programme," wrote Pierre Lalo, the French critic. The financial crisis was so bad that Mahler himself had to plead with Baron Albert de Rothschild for money to pay the musicians' journey home.

Despite his great success with the classics, in particular Beethoven, despite the novelties (Mahler's penultimate concert was the first performance of *Das klagende Lied* on 17 February 1901, in Vienna), the Orchestra's resistance to Mahler's "tyrannical" strictness grew and the differences of opinion became more frequent.

He was not able to conduct either of the last two subscription concerts because of his failing health. They were conducted by Josef Hellmesberger Jr and Franz Schalk. The critics praised the "classical tradition"; nothing like it had been heard since Richter's time. Soon after Mahler's provisional resignation came the final one in April 1901, the reason being that because of the amount of work and his ill-health "it will henceforth be impossible for me to assume the conductorship of the Philharmonic Concerts". This was how the feeling of aversion, which had arisen through disagreement and which could no longer be concealed, was described. Perhaps there was something which might have kept him there: unanimous re-election which the committee could guarantee. The musicians, who were tired of authoritarianism, selected the accommodating, mediocre Josef Hellmesberger Jr to be his successor.

If one reflects on the fact that during these three seasons Mahler conducted 240 performances in the Opera House and 36 performances of the Vienna Philharmonic Orchestra, and if one includes his fanaticism about rehearsals, the question remains: when did he ever manage to compose?

He acted as guest conductor for the Vienna Philharmonic until 1907 on six further occasions, including two performances of his *Third Symphony* and on 7 December 1905 the first performance of his *Fifth Symphony* and, at his farewell concert in Vienna on 24 November 1907, he conducted his *Second Symphony*.

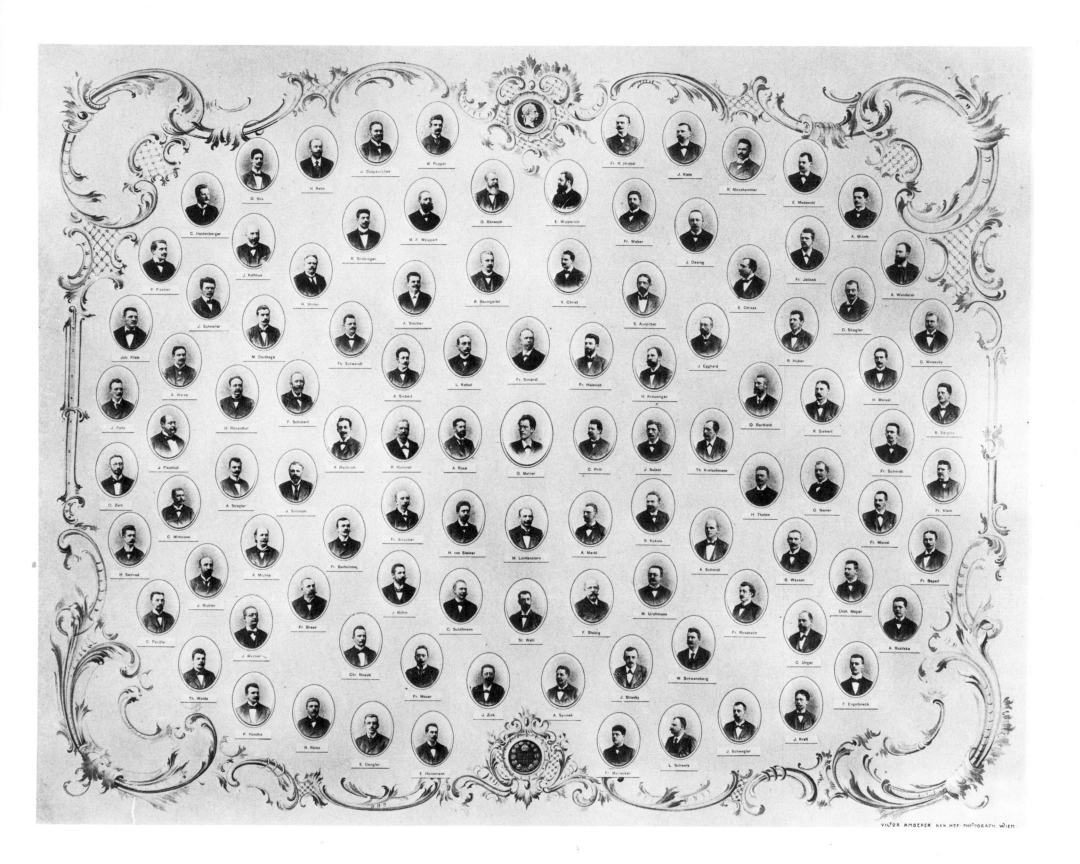

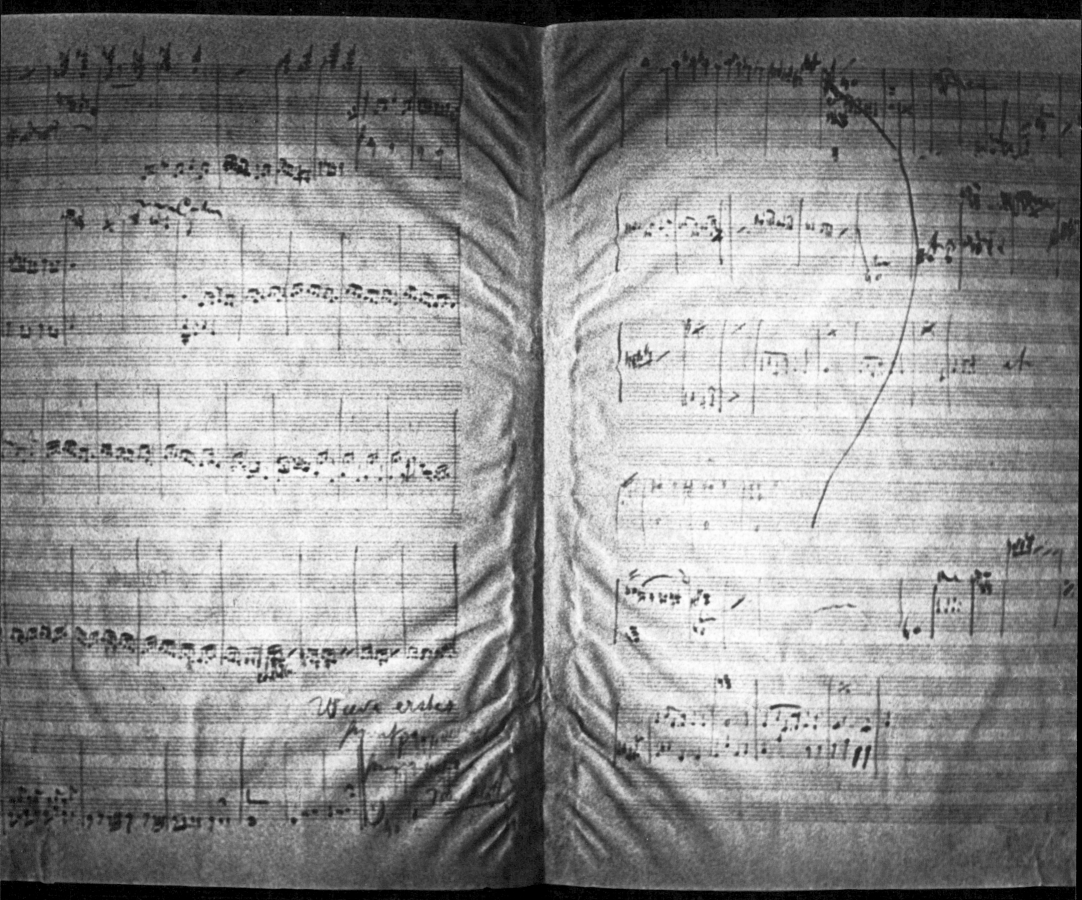

Friedrich C. Heller

GUSTAV MAHLER'S CREATIVE WORK IN HIS VIENNA YEARS

After his first efforts (which were mostly fragmentary and later destroyed) Gustav Mahler's creative work was very soon concentrated into only two spheres: the lied and the symphony. With this specialization, which combines the simplest vocal form with the most extensive instrumental combination, the intention at the back of his musical language also becomes clear: to draw the innermost lyricism and intimate expression of lyric form into the epic narrative possibilities of orchestral music. As a logical result Mahler's lied with piano accompaniment was expanded into the lied with orchestral accompaniment, and the symphony became enriched with lied elements. Judged by the number of works, his œuvre is not large, but if one keeps in mind the spiritual content it appears infinitely extensive. In addition it is the narrow idealistic and musical connection between the works themselves which expresses itself in an abundance of self-quotations and ever-recurring characteristic melodic types and bears witness to Mahler's remark: "The term 'symphony' – to me this means creating a world with all the technical means available."

With this sort of perception, Mahler stands without question in a tradition which derives from Beethoven and which, following the 19th century form of aesthetic expression, transformed the "absolute music" of the classical symphony into a work

Left: Sketches for the *Third Symphony* dating from 1896.

129

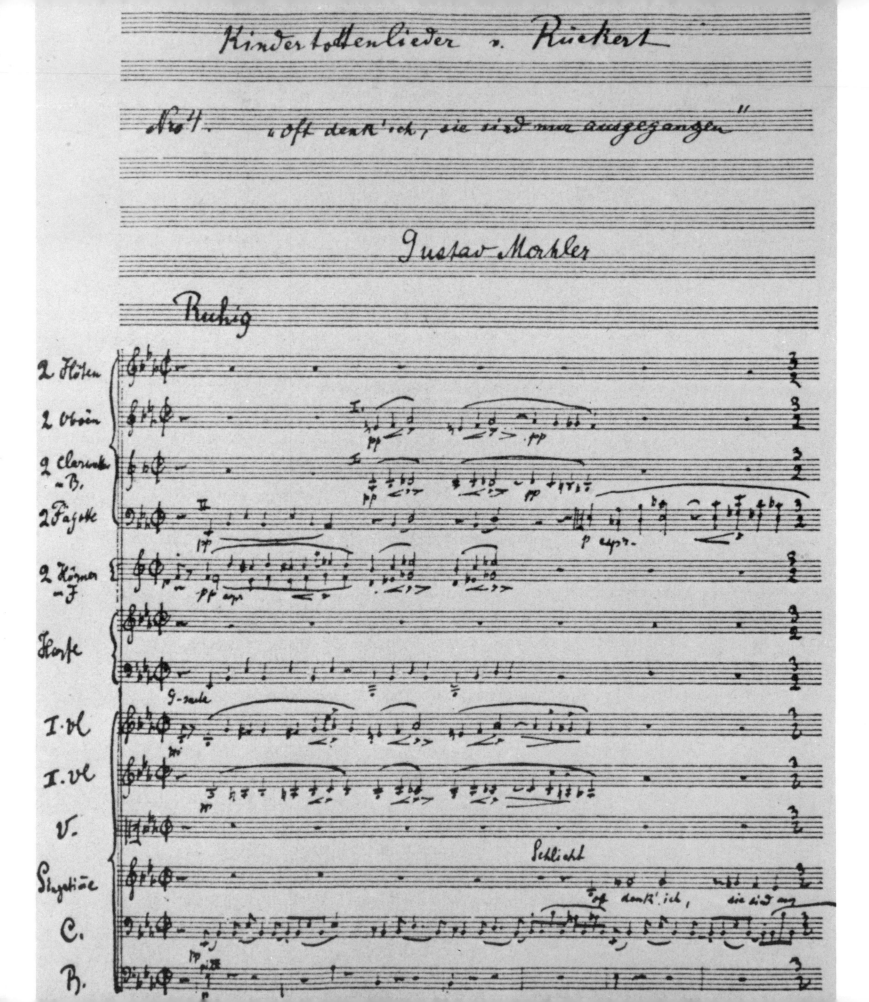

of personal creed. The spiritual power of the artist is reflected in Mahler, who in his individuality, as in a focal point, also collects the rational and emotional streams and movements of his time, the hopes and yearnings, the suffering and the love. Out of his type of personal creed, which submits only with difficulty to the aesthetic and stylistic rules of its period, the wish to convey a message also emerges. Beethoven's *Ninth Symphony* proclaimed the praise of joy: his *Missa Solemnis* "came from the heart" and wanted to "return to the heart". Mahler's *Eighth Symphony* was intended to be a gift to the whole nation. "Creating a world for myself" turned into "for you". The artist, who was striving for possibilities of salvation, wanted to let his fellow men (whom, as has been attested several times, he considered his brothers) share his doubts and fears, his memories and religious visions.

In Mahler's lifetime this missionary creed was accepted by only a small number of followers; those who were convinced, however, revered him as a saint. Schönberg, Berg and Webern, for example, thought of Mahler as someone of overwhelming greatness. That which was perhaps more a presentiment or was still influenced by the personal encounter, has grown now, half a century later, into an obviously worldwide experience. Nowadays Mahler's music, despite the fact that it is by no means easy to perform, is an established fact in the musical world. The former polemical discussion has changed into an ever more deeply urgent one, especially among young people. This can be explained not only as being a new "nostalgic" consciousness, but rather it seems as if Mahler's saying that his music was an "anticipation" of the after life had proved true. The listener today may feel, consciously or intuitively, that it is our world which speaks to him through Mahler's music, that it is our world with its beauty and increasing disintegration and that it is therefore "his" music.

If one tries to classify Mahler's music according to the place of origin, the most extensive part would come during the Vienna years, from 1897 to 1907. But this is only part of the story: as described elsewhere, Mahler's composing was done mostly during the summer months and therefore at his summer retreat in the country; only there was he able to cut himself off from the world in the literal and figurative sense which he needed for his creative work. During the Vienna Opera season, there remained only time for the exceedingly complicated orchestration and preparation of the score, a work process which, considering how very exacting the particular sound constructions he wished to realize in his music were, certainly made considerable demands on him. After his marriage to Alma Schindler, herself a trained musician, she was able to help him in many ways.

If, then, it does not at first seem wholly justified to speak of the work of the "Vienna Years", one must consider that with such a far-reaching spirit as Mahler's one cannot very easily quote geographical arguments. It is a matter of clarifying certain aspects and features of his music. Without doubt the musical climate in Vienna had a lasting effect on Mahler and what he gave shape to in the direct creative process elsewhere in the summer months was supplied by the source whence his human and artistic personality drew its stimuli and conception. Mahler, the thinker and the man who, like so many of his time, felt the enormous and fascinating influence of the philosophy of Friedrich Nietzsche, was nevertheless striving in apparently repeatedly new expositions for a Christian conception of the world which could be realized in ethical terms. Mahler anticipated a way of self-realization in co-suffering (just as he found it imposingly portrayed in the works of Dostoievsky). He thought he would find the fulfilment of his post-Romantic longings in the ironic many-sided poetry of Jean Paul and then in the simple sentimental world of the *Wunderhorn* poetry (fulfilment which finally led to conscious resignation in which Goethe's neo-platonism and Eastern fatalism must have had a determinative effect). All this built up within the artist an inexplicable complex sensitivity, at the same time extravagant and

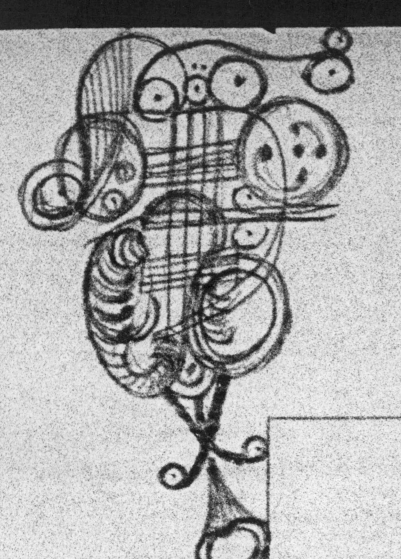

Telegramm.

Telegraphenamt:

Zur Nachricht: Durch Einwurf in Briefsammelkasten aufgegebene Telegramme müssen durch den Absender mit Postfrankomarken im tarifmäßigen Betrage frankiert sein. Die Aufgabeblankette müssen in diesem Falle in Briefform gefaltet sein, dürfen aber nicht fest verschlossen werden.

vulnerable, which was always generous and yet likely to become withdrawn and "lost to the world".

Mahler's far-reaching spirit, which expressed itself in many of his letters but above all in his work, cannot be subordinated to the sphere of influence of a particular place. But the historical and cultural aura of Vienna at any rate was so many-sided and so complex that a receptive artist of this sort and of such variety could feel more than usually inspired here. The student of the Conservatory felt this just as much as the mature man. Moreover, through his young wife, Mahler came into contact with the pictorial arts. The daughter of Emil Jakob Schindler, the painter, and a friend of Gustav Klimt, she opened the way for the musician and opera director to the artistic circle of the Vienna Secession. Mahler participated in several of the events organized by this group of artists. His private life included the friendship of some of them and in the congenial Alfred Roller, a member of the Secession, he found the man who realized his opera dramaturgy.

The question arises as to what extent the prevailing *Jugendstil* influence can be recognized in Mahler's music itself, and whether, as with the Secession, it was a matter of a specific Viennese variant. For the musicologist today this question still cannot be properly answered because the phenomenon of the musical *Jugendstil* has been only inadequately defined and investigated. A parallel nonetheless could be possibly discerned in Mahler's fondness for the romantic poetry in the *Des Knaben Wunderhorn* collection (he used fourteen of the text for lieder) and, in his own verses, the *Lieder eines fahrenden Gesellen*, he clearly sympathized with their mood and language. This recalls the tendency of the German and Austrian *Jugendstil* to imitate Biedermeier forms, for example in the popular architecture of private houses and gardens. This comparison merely appears to conceal the national longing for a "simple and beautiful, good and sad world"; this sort of nostalgia which evolved during the 19th century could be a major background element in both Mahler and *Jugendstil*. An attempt was made to link many of the characteristics in the text of *Das Lied von der Erde* with concepts about the current direction in which art was moving at the time, but all these interpretations concern only superficialities. The nucleus of the question, the essence of the music, must for the time being remain unanswered. It may be that certain melodic phrases of Mahler's music reflect the essence of one aspect of *Jugendstil* (though not that of Vienna), as has occasionally been established, but even this comparison only touches the surface of the music.

The Viennese musical tradition was possibly important in another way in view of Mahler's period of study with Robert Fuchs. The importance of this teacher in regard

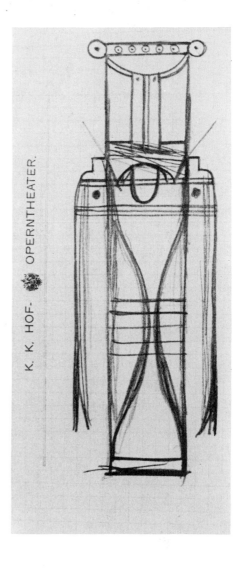

Gustav Mahler's scribblings on a telegram form and one of the opera house letter-cards (see p. 83). Alfred Roller took these "by-products" and kept them.

135

Sheet from the Adagio of the *Fourth Symphony*.

to Mahler's early style requires further investigation. Fuchs, after all, also taught Mahler's contemporary and colleague Hugo Wolf, and among his later pupils were Franz Schreker and several composers of operetta. Mahler also attended Anton Bruckner's lectures at the University (without actually being his "teacher" Bruckner exerted a considerable influence on Mahler). Guido Adler, the eminent musicologist, was one of his early Viennese friends.

These personal encounters, just as much as the overall musical ambience of the city, had a decided effect on Mahler's composition – but only so far as the many-sided structure of his inner life, based on innate self-confidence, would allow.

It is now time to mention the works which were composed in the Vienna years between 1897 and 1907. These are two lieder (with texts from *Des Knaben Wunderhorn*), *Revelge*, and *Der Tamboursg'sell* (1899), the *Fourth Symphony* (1899–1900), *Die Kindertotenlieder* based on texts by Friedrich Rückert, five other songs on texts by Rückert (subsequently called *Lieder aus letzter Zeit* which were written between 1901 and 1902), the *Fifth Symphony* (1901–2), the *Sixth Symphony* (1903–4), the *Seventh Symphony* (1904–5), and finally, the *Eighth Symphony* (1906–7). An impressive volume of composition if one considers Mahler's enormous involvement as operatic director and conductor. Within the range of the symphonies listed the transition takes place from the world of the *Wunderhorn* poetry (which still had a profound effect on the *Fourth Symphony*) to a form of expression which in three symphonies makes use of the instrumental resources alone, and finally, in the *Eighth Symphony*, uses an enormous vocal and instrumental ensemble to bring to life its equally colossal spiritual vision.

But these sorts of divisions – which reflect the usual classification of Mahler's work – affect only the surface of the music. What is more important is the inner development of his composition. It can be alluded to here only briefly: in two interlinked developments Mahler dispenses with the noticeably clear tonal basis of the melodic and harmonic structure which was still perceptible in earlier works as well as the clearly constructed homophonic style of previous years. This development ends with the complete abandonment of tonality and the collapse of the traditional forms.

Mahler did not completely achieve either, his early death prevented this, but there are enough signs which point in this direction. In many details which still have to be examined but which are characteristic of his later style, Mahler's music shows itself to be the direct forerunner of the music of our century. More than that of other masters at the turn of the century, his work affected not only the succeeding generation (for example Berg and Webern), but especially the young composers after 1950.

The proximity of order and chaos, which distinguishes his music more and more, particularly after the *Fifth Symphony*, acquired an overwhelming symbolic and impressive power for our century; it is shown in the "collage" type juxtaposition of totally different materials.

That Mahler's contemporaries were not able to understand or even accept the meaning of this way of composing seems almost intelligible. They were not yet so far ahead in the experience of the destructibility of all types of the old order as some artists.

In the *Fourth Symphony* there is as yet hardly anything of such a world to be seen. Its gaiety and almost childlike naturalness concludes the first epoch of striving in which Mahler had searched for answers to the question of salvation (in the *First, Second* and *Third Symphonies*). In the *Fourth Symphony* a more elevated point of view seems to have been attained: it is the gentle good humour that gives this music, in which Mahler rejects the use of an over-large orchestra, its happy style. Many have attempted to recognize in it classical sounds but it does not require any such allusions. The *Fourth Symphony* is among Mahler's most popular works, probably because it so unquestioningly demonstrates a beautiful world, a world, however, which one suspects does not yet exist here, though it does exist elsewhere, in the "heavenly life"; the final movement hints at this. Here the type of music such as in the second movement *Freund Hein Spielt Auf* ("Death Plays On"), does not develop into a

The last page of the lied "Look not, love, on my work unended" (*4 Rückert Lieder*). It was finished on 14 June 1901.

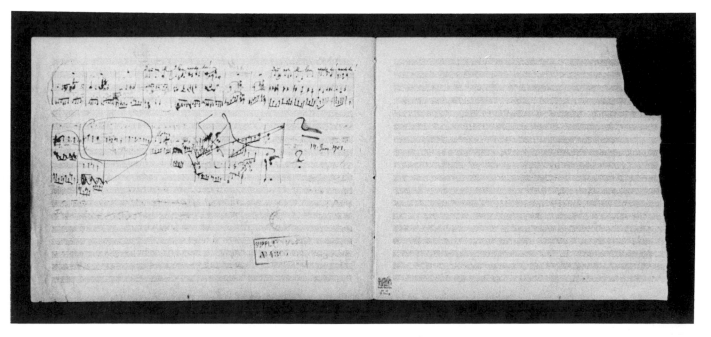

Two pages from the original score of the *Eighth Symphony*, second movement (composed in 1906 and 1907).

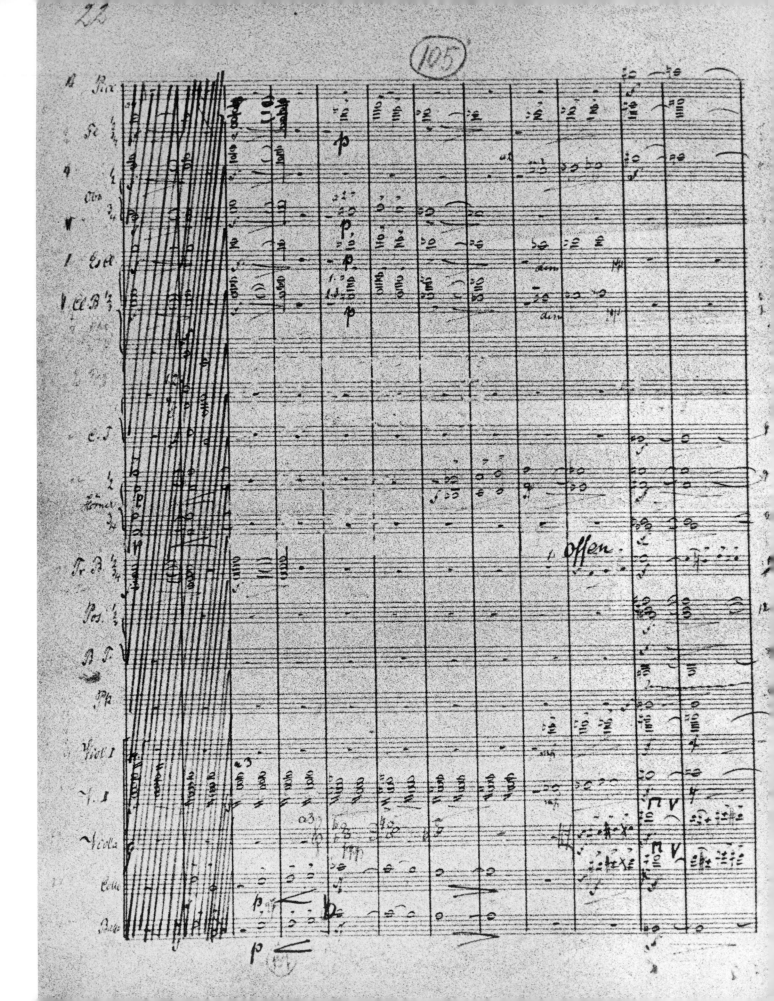

23.
Mater gloriosa schwebt einher
Rit.
Sehr langsam
Schwächstes Register
pp
I. Solo
2 Harf.
col Harfen

serious piece, rather a parodying caricature which one simply accepts as a deliberate contrast.

The introversion of the inner self and the necessity of expressing the two conflicting sides of his character led Mahler away from the pleasant vague sadness of a bourgeois century which was drawing to a close. He found the lyricism, which made possible the self-expression, in the poems of Friedrich Rückert. The culmination came in the famous *Kindertotenlieder* and in the dreamy "I am lost to the world" (from the *Lieder aus letzter Zeit*) of which the composer said "It is I myself". Even in music a new field of expression inevitably leads to new technical innovations. Mahler was wholly conscious of this new start.

In 1911, the year of his death, having finished the second revision of his *Fifth Symphony*, he confessed: "It is inconceivable to me how, at that time, I managed to be so completely wrong again, just like a beginner. Apparently the routine I had acquired in the first four Symphonies had let me down totally – because a new style demanded a completely new technique." This new style led to the purely instrumental symphony. In three large-scale works a very large orchestra is used, but naturally with an increasingly differentiating orchestration. The objective is not primarily a "beautiful" or an "interesting" timbre, rather a clear and transparent structure, a technique which became important in 20th century music. The result is a growing clarity of the musical design. Moreover, it combines a free use of counterpoint.

During the first years of this century, Mahler occupied himself exhaustively with the compositions of Johann Sebastian Bach. The *Kindertotenlieder* and the *Fifth Symphony* show the first result of this preoccupation with the technique of several voices led along in polyphony. Right up to the end it became the distinguishing mark of Mahler's later works. But this counterpoint no longer conforms to the school rules. It assumes the notion of making each voice-line independent of the others, but is not carried through in a firm framework with a tonal centre.

Thus we have some passages, such as at the beginning of the second movement in the *Fifth Symphony*, where the melodic construction threatens to collapse into several fragments which alternate and intermingle. The breakdown of the traditional language has begun and cannot be ignored. It does not have to show itself simply by disintegration. Compositions such as the lied *Ich atmet' einen linden Duft* (from the *Lieder aus letzter Zeit*), in which the vocal line, contrary to the original function of singing, is embedded in the linear texture demonstrates the way in which, in many places, conventional musical thinking was becoming extensively alienated. There are

The title page to the first edition of the *Eighth Symphony*, which appeared in 1911.

Thomas Mann became acquainted with Mahler at the world première of the *Eighth Symphony* in Munich. Katja Mann recalls in her reminiscences that Thomas Mann said to her: "Indeed, that was the first time in my life that I had the feeling that I had met a really great man." On 13 September 1910 he wrote to Mahler: "I was not able, during the evening at the hotel, to tell you how deeply I am in your debt for the impressions of 12 September. I feel compelled however to give you some idea and so I would like you to accept a copy of the enclosed book (*Königliche Hoheit*) – my latest. Obviously it is scarcely suitable as a quid pro quo for what I have received from you and must weigh almost nothing in the hand of the man in whom, as I firmly believe, is embodied the most serious, the most saintly artistic determination of our time..."
Right: Rehearsal for the first performance of the *Eighth Symphony* in the Odeon-Saal, Munich, in September 1910.

vigorous parts which abound in expressive power (as in the *Fifth* and *Seventh Symphonies*) placed next to funeral marches and introverted, calm episodes of indescribable tranquillity in the same symphonies. Incompatabilities appear to thrive in many cases with common motifs and yet are as far apart as two strange worlds. In the finale the *Fifth Symphony* resolves itself into a blaze of triumph – this is unmistakably demonstrated by a choral theme. In the *Sixth Symphony*, rightly called *The Tragic*, there is a further prophetic allusion to the idea of catastrophe interspersed with idyllic episodes and recollections. The finale crashes over the listener like dissonant destruction, the terrible hammerblow that finally resounds, immediately becoming quieter, does not catch one unawares, but is nonetheless painful in its deathly powerlessness. It is hard to believe that after such music there could be a pathway upwards towards a better world.

But, however one wishes to correlate Mahler's development as a composer with the circumstances of his life, it is more important to recognize that the negation, as it is manifested in the finale of the *Sixth Symphony*, is placed on an equal footing with the affirmation of triumphant life, and only the two together result in the whole world of these works.

This may explain the excitement which permeates the *Seventh Symphony* as a great feeling which sweeps everything with it, as if, by experiencing tragedy, the good forces were released.

This joyous impulse brings us to the crowning glory of this group of symphonies, the *Eighth*, in which the incompatible seems to have become reconciled in the imploring words of the *Pentecost Hymn*, in the plea for enlightenment which makes up this text as much as in the long passage from the closing scene of Goethe's *Faust*, in the mysterious representation of love which finally draws us upwards and in whose light "All things transitory are but a parable". Mahler banished the redeeming significance of calamity and made it part of all-embracing love. The enormous forces used in this symphony, which is written for choirs, soloists, and a very large orchestra, are nonetheless used with extraordinary sensitivity. Where, however, the forces in their entirety are heard, the very size of the concept is convincing. The appeal of the spirit and of love is unlimited.

The *Sixth* and the *Eighth Symphonies* are poles apart. It was no longer possible to progress further in either direction. Therefore the later works of Mahler, composed after the Vienna period (*Das Lied von der Erde*, the *Ninth Symphony* and the fragment of the *Tenth Symphony*), ended in the resignation of a man bound to reality. Perhaps the departure from Vienna, the city in which he had lived to see the great-

Gustav Mahler in Amsterdam with Alphons Diepenbrock and Willem Mengelberg (first and second from the left). Mengelberg was one of the earliest and most important promoters of Gustav Mahler's compositions.
Right: The last page of the original manuscript orchestral score of the *Fourth Symphony*.

est activity of his career and where he also experienced the greatest hostility, had given Mahler the feeling that he must accept what was to come without the possibility of a superhuman creed. With the acceptance of reality the music finally fades into silence.

arco

ppp

morendo

Ende der Symphonie

Euer Hochwolgeboren!

Die Verehrer Gustav Mahlers versammeln sich zum Abschied am **Montag d. 9. vor ½ 9 Uhr früh am Perron des Westbahnhofs** und laden Sie ein, dort zu erscheinen und Gleichgesinnte davon zu verständigen. Da Mahler mit dieser Kundgebung überrascht werden soll, erscheint es dringend geboten, Personen, die der Presse nahestehen, nicht ins Vertrauen zu ziehen.

Dr. Anton v. Webern. **Dr. Paul Stefan.**
Dr. Karl Horwitz. **Heinrich Jalowetz.**

Wolf Rosenberg

GUSTAV MAHLER'S FAREWELL AND RETURN HOME

USA – the land of "impossible limitations", as Busoni used to say. Did Mahler feel like an expatriate there? At the time friends and adversaries appeared to have formed a secret alliance: they started a rumour that the former conductor of the Vienna Opera was already regretting having staked his job so recklessly, that he was consumed with yearning for his beloved Vienna, that he was withering away in the American cultural void. Some parts of his letters appear to confirm this, others indicate the opposite. For once in a way, the truth may well lie in the middle or even consist of two half-truths; Mahler was not only capable of extreme reactions, he was also well able to consider things clear-headedly and, after all, he went into exile of his own free will.

In December 1907 when he crossed the ocean for the first time, he had signed a four-year contract with the Metropolitan Opera: he served two years (between four and five months in each case) and for the remaining two years he was principal conductor of the New York Philharmonic Orchestra. His aim was to earn money so that he would finally be able to compose in peace. (The fact that he never achieved that "peace", that he frankly needed the friction of everyday musical life, is another matter.)

Left: Gustav Mahler in 1907.

Programme leaflet of one of the New York Philharmonic concerts conducted by Gustav Mahler during the 1910/1911 season. Right: Gustav Mahler in New York 1909.

Mahler was even prepared to make concessions up to a point. But this does not mean that he had conceived his work as a necessary evil or had fulfilled his obligations in a listless way. He had hardly arrived, had hardly realized how hopelessly antiquated the productions were, when he was already trying to convince the authorities in charge of the Met that Alfred Roller would have to be sent for from Vienna – "the only one who can pull the cart out of the mud both artistically and personally."

Following the failure of this plan – obviously some of the people in New York were as good at intriguing as their counterparts in Vienna – he at least managed to get the stage sets for the new production of *Fidelio* modelled on Roller's Vienna sets.

Mahler was also able to arrange for more rehearsal time than had been customary at the Metropolitan Opera, even if it was not as much as he was used to in Vienna. And he must have had less trouble with the solo ensembles, at least musically, but to what extent he bothered about the production is almost impossible to say. There was an excellent cast available for the Mozart operas (*Don Giovanni* in the first season and *Figaro* in the second): Johanna Gadski, Emma Eames, Geraldine Farrar, Marcella Sembrich, Bonci, Scotti, Didur, Chaliapin; for the Wagner operas (*Tristan*, *Walküre* and *Siegfried*) he had such great singers as Olive Fremstad, Anton van Rooy, Burrian, Knote, etc. He had evidently overcome his scepticism about the lustre of great names and it should also be borne in mind that in those days the market value of a singer was in most cases in keeping with his artistic quality or, to put it more prudently, singers who were purely vocal athletes could not expect to get top fees and at best would only sing on stages in the provinces.

Mahler experienced happy surprises as well as grievous disappointments. What he wrote in a letter to Alfred Roller may sound exaggeratedly euphoric: "The public here and all the factors which an artist has to consider – not least the directors themselves (mostly multi-millionaires) – are spoiled and misled but – in contrast to 'our people' in Vienna (and by that I also mean the Aryan gentlemen) – not at all conceited, greedy for all that is new and incredibly eager to learn… The people here are tremendously vigorous – all rawness and unenlightened – still suffering from children's diseases…"

This was only a few weeks after his arrival and later statements sound much less optimistic. Without doubt, increasing exasperation with the system was becoming noticeable, one which was hardly more flexible than that in Vienna, although the conditions were probably somewhat more favourable. Instead of having to battle against an imperial bureaucracy, Mahler merely had to fight against half a dozen rich patrons.

New York in 1907.

Consequently he refused to succeed Conried, manager of the Met, who was to relinquish his office at the start of the 1908/09 season. The fact that he had to be careful of his health after the Viennese doctors had diagnosed a valvular heart defect may have been a contributory factor. Or was the musical direction of an opera house too tiring?

Certainly there were disappointments, but not only those about which Alma so ingenuously fabricated stories. Gatti-Casazza, who became the new manager of the Met, brought Toscanini with him from Milan. The latter caused Mahler frightful vexation. This is how Alma put it in her reminiscences: "Toscanini had stipulated in the contract that he would conduct the first performance of *Tristan* – the *Tristan* which Mahler had been rehearsing! Mahler, tired of fighting, had handed over *Tristan* whereupon Toscanini immediately completely re-rehearsed Mahler's new interpretation. This was a great insult to Mahler and all his enjoyment of the Opera House in New York vanished. Everyone had read the telegrams which had been exchanged between the Metropolitan and Gatti-Casazza in order to engage Toscanini. As his most important objective and as a condition of the engagement, Toscanini demanded that he be given *Tristan* and Mahler handed the work over to him. No word of thanks. From the first glance, Mahler was disdainfully ignored." The only thing which is true in all this is that Toscanini wanted to introduce himself to the New Yorkers with *Tristan*.

But Mahler raised objections. In a letter to the authorities in New York we read, "I put a great deal of effort into *Tristan* in the previous season and can indeed claim that the form in which this work is now appearing in New York is my spiritual property. If Toscanini, for whom I have the greatest respect, although I don't know him personally (and it is an honour for me to welcome him as a colleague), were now to take over *Tristan* before my season's entry, the work would be imprinted with a totally different stamp and it would be quite impossible for me to take over the work during the later course of the season. I must therefore urgently request that the direction of this work should be reserved for me and that accordingly it should not be included in the repertory before 17 December."

At this, Toscanini waived his contractual rights, selected *Aida* for the first performance and took over *Tristan* only in 1910, at a time when Mahler had already transferred to the Philharmonic Orchestra and conducted only as a guest at the Met (four performances of Tchaikovsky's *Queen of Spades*, with Emmy Destinn and Leo Slezak). Toscanini had rejected the remark about having "disdainfully ignored" Mahler as being malicious. It is perfectly possible that he may have behaved in a re-

Gustav Mahler during his last journey to New York in November 1910.

Composer's signet on the facsimile edition of the sketches for the *Tenth Symphony* (Vienna 1924).
Right: Mahler's notes on the sketch pages for the *Tenth Symphony*.

served manner towards Mahler, but probably less because of the dispute over *Tristan* than out of a sense of disappointment.

Harold C. Schonberg is subsequently supposed to have explained that one of the reasons why Toscanini went to the Met was that so great a musician as Mahler was working there; however, he soon realized that Mahler was not working wholeheartedly and made things too easy for himself. Actually in some respects Mahler had become easy-going; whereas in Vienna he had raged against everyone who made cuts in Wagner's works, he was now performing an abbreviated *Tristan* and because of his health he was probably no longer rehearsing with his former fanaticism.

However, even if rumours were circulating in Vienna that he was only "cashing in", that he was no longer concerned about the standard of his performances and was leading a life of luxury, they had as little justification as the gossip which implied that after taking over the New York Philharmonic he had slipped into an inferior job, as though a concert conductor counted for less than an opera conductor.

In a letter to Guido Adler dated 1 January 1910, Mahler put things in their proper perspective: "Practical activity is absolutely essential for my musical ability to counteract the enormous inner experiences when composing: and conducting a concert orchestra is something I have been wanting to do all my life. I am glad to have been able to enjoy this once in my life (in addition I am learning something from it, because theatre technique is quite different and I am convinced that many of my former shortcomings in orchestration are attributable to the fact that I am accustomed to listening under the totally different conditions of the theatre). Why has not Germany or Austria offered me something like this? Is it my fault that Vienna threw me out? And anyway I need a certain amount of luxury, a comfortable way of life which my pension (the only thing I was to acquire in almost thirty years of conducting) would not have permitted. So for me it is a welcome way out that America has now offered me; it is not only the type of activity which suits my inclinations and abilities, but it also carries adequate compensation which will soon put me in a position to enjoy, in a dignified way, as much of the evening of my life as is allotted to me."

As we know, there was no evening to his life, but plenty of legends about his work in America continued to be born. In 1921 Ludwig Karpath, a Viennese critic, published an article in which he threw light upon Mahler's work in America under the nationalistic Viennese aspect, so to speak. The subtly concealed message ran: We clever Viennese knew what Mahler meant to us, whereas the Americans treated him badly. Actually it serves him right.

IV

Scherzo

Der Teufel tanzt es mit mir

Wahnsin, fass mich an, Verfluchten!

vernichte mich
dass ich vergesse, dass ich bin!
dass ich aufhöre, zu sein

dass ich ver

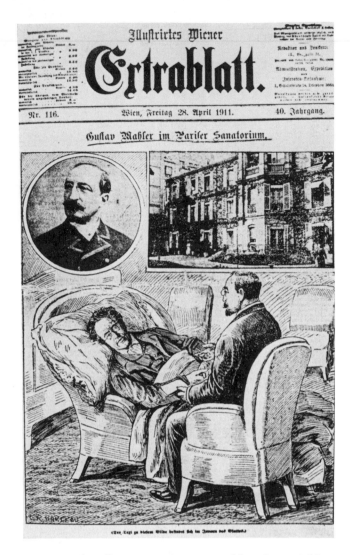

Report in the *Illustriertes Wiener Extrablatt* about Mahler's illness in April 1911.
Right: The first page of the Finale sketch from the *Tenth Symphony* which Mahler never finished.

"In the theatre he was simply looked upon as the Kapellmeister, certainly not as a top-flight artist though he had been honoured as such…"

The thesis was, more or less, that he had no success in America and as chief witness a New York "superior" (Mahler's pet name for music critics), Henry Krehbiel of the *Tribune*, is quoted as saying in an obituary after Mahler's death that his American career was not a success.

Indeed, according to Krehbiel and to other New York and Viennese critics Mahler was unsuccessful, and if Krehbiel had read the newspaper articles by Helm or Hirschfeld he could without hesitation have added: his Austrian career was not successful either. Of course, here and there Mahler was unsuccessful to the extent that he was not universally acclaimed and that he was "inconvenient" to many people; on the other hand, he was more than successful because he shocked some and thrilled others. No one took him for an average Kapellmeister even if some critics did try to create this impression and the vehement pro and contra arguments which he caused in New York as well as in Vienna confirmed his standing. Moreover, as a concert conductor he succeeded in making himself unpopular by presenting unconventional programmes.

Another New York critic, Henry T. Finck, wrote with touching naïveté: "Although Mahler was a first-rate conductor, he did not know how to put together a programme which would attract the public. Above all, he despised and neglected Tchaikovsky, the favourite symphonic composer of the concertgoer. Subscription sales were affected. Stransky [Mahler's successor] had the same taste as the public and one of the reasons for his popularity was that he didn't banish any first class works from his programmes simply because they were popular."

"Money talks", was a piece of critic Krehbiel's worldly wisdom and indeed, whereas Mahler often did not succeed in filling the house, because he favoured composers such as Bach, Mozart, Schumann and Bruckner, and included many novelties in his programmes, Stransky managed to treble the subscriptions in the course of a decade by including Grieg, Tchaikovsky, Dvorak, Rimsky-Korsakov and others.

But just as there were friends and enemies among the critics, so too, the "public" was not a homogeneous mass. Those people who came to Mahler's concerts, although Tchaikovsky was seldom heard and the concert hall was seldom full, were in his mind when he wrote: "The audiences here are very kind and, compared with Vienna, relatively respectable. They listen attentively and with goodwill." This chapter in Mahler's life is still not completely explained even today. There is far too little source material, but an abundance of conscious or unconscious falsehoods, de-

Was gibt's denn Neues?

Gustav Mahler †.

Die Trauer der Hofoper.

Obwohl man in der Hofoper auf den Eintritt der Katastrophe vorbereitet war, erregte doch die Trauerkunde in allen Kreisen des Instituts starke, allgemeine Teilnahme. Man hatte Mahler als Chef immer die gebührende Hochachtung und Wertschätzung entgegengebracht und alle Weiterungen blieben außer Stande, die großen Sympathien herabzumindern, die man dem genialen Leiter des Institutes zollte. Mahler war es, der den Mitgliedern des Hofopernorchesters den Titel „Hofmusiker" erkämpfte; er erwirkte Verbesserungen der wirtschaftlichen Lage des Chores und technischen Personales und berechtigte Anforderungen des Künstlerensembles fanden an Mahler stets einen bereiten Anwalt.

Direktor Gregor hat heute vormittags folgende Kurrende hinausgegeben:

Ich erfülle die schmerzliche Pflicht, die Mitglieder des k. k. Hofoperntheaters von dem Ableben Gustav Mahlers in Kenntnis zu setzen.

Das Andenken dieses Mannes wird in diesem Hause nie untergehen.

Tag und Stunde der Bestattung und ihre näheren Umstände werden rechtzeitig bekanntgegeben werden.

The death notice in a Viennese daily paper.
Right: Arnold Schönberg's picture of Gustav Mahler's funeral (oil painting dating from 1911).

ceptions and legends. Much of this has been corrected by Kurt Blaukopf, much more will certainly be put right in the second volume of Henri-Louis de La Grange's comprehensive biography of Mahler.

After Mahler had to break off his concert activity prematurely in February 1911 when he was already mortally ill and had returned to Europe, he attained a certain degree of popularity in Vienna. More active interest was shown to the dying Mahler than to the healthy, active man. The bulletins in the newspapers became more frequent, firstly from Paris. "No notable change in Mahler's condition. There is little fever today though he has a much faster pulse" ran the somewhat sparse statement on 25 April. One day later two bulletins were issued, then a more detailed one from Vienna and as a precaution, the obituaries were already being sent to the printers – a fact which Karl Kraus criticized in the *Fackel* issue of June 1911: "The obituary notice must be written long before the actual death – it is inherent in the profession – so that it can appear directly after death; and a newspaper which erroneously allows it to appear before the death always enjoys more respect than one which only publishes it afterwards. Those who are devoted to the profession take the odium of it upon themselves. The journalistic coffins must be prepared in advance and the reader does not wait as long as the gravedigger. He who wants to belong to that concordia, which buries the corpses more quickly, may not shrink from the idea that he might one day need to sit down with the telephone in one hand to answer a newspaper subscriber: 'Mahler is better'; while writing with the other: 'Mahler is dead'. If it is not absolutely necessary nobody will choose this profession [journalism]. It is no less contemptible in a time of enlightenment than that of the hangman. Social necessities are – necessary. The only people who are contemptible are those who voluntarily place themselves at the service of such people who are paid for it... The Court theatre directors who published obituaries of Gustav Mahler in the Friday morning issue of *Neue Freie Presse*, when he died at 11.05 p.m. on the Thursday, are contemptible. The Court theatre authorities should immediately ask Messrs. Gregor and Berger what the sequence of events was. The authorities should ask Herr Gregor at what time – between five minutes past eleven and the time the type was set for the morning paper (assuming that he heard about Mahler's death at the very same minute) – he had written this sentence: 'Now inexorable fate has killed him!' At what time had he reflected about the universe, about the districts where our law of causality ends? (I believe these are all the districts in Greater Vienna.) When had he uttered the profoundly modest notion that 'we experience emptiness where Mahler once had been'?"

In his pamphlet Kraus quoted the music reviewer who wrote the obituary in the *Neues Wiener Tagblatt:* "Our space is much too restricted for us to go more deeply into the real meaning of Mahler as a composer."

Even in the concert halls people were in this respect apparently much too inhibited. Vienna could have said more about the significance of Mahler the composer by offering a first performance of *Das Lied von der Erde,* but this privilege was left to the people of Munich (November 1911 under Bruno Walter). All the same, they made sure of the *Ninth Symphony* (June 1912, also conducted by Walter) and *Das Lied von der Erde* was heard several times in Vienna in the next few years.

After 1918 it looked for a while as if Mahler's time had come: the number of performances increased, in 1920 Oskar Fried conducted an almost complete Mahler cycle (all the symphonies except the *Eighth*). But, during the twenties, interest waned again, at least in official music circles, whereas at the workers' symphony concerts, whose programmes had for a long time, even before Anton Webern took over the musical direction, been much more progressive and colourful than those of the Vienna Philharmonic Orchestra, Mahler's work was kept alive.

After 1945 the "return" set in, though rather faint-heartedly at first. There was a revival of interest with the founding of the International Mahler Society and the new edition of his works; in 1960, the hundredth anniversary of Mahler's birth, there was a remarkable exhibition: "Mahler and his times", and the Austrian radio broadcast all the symphonies with a brilliant choice of conductors: Josef Krips, Bruno Walter, Dimitri Mitropoulos, Hans Swarowsky, Michael Gielen, Winfried Zillig – all top-flight Mahler specialists.

The *Gesamtzyklus* was organized by the *Konzerthausgesellschaft* in 1967, and apart from Swarowsky, in particular Abbado, Maderna and Carlos Kleiber also made invaluable contributions to the present-day reception of Mahler.

But, despite all this, has the "return" really been achieved? Will the unusual in Mahler's music – not just its merit – be recognized? Will we really occupy ourselves with his work or will it simply be consumed? A nightmare has come true: Mahler has become a brand article. He is traded in every shape, in every type of packaging, depending on taste.

I found what is today a rather charmingly Utopian remark about Mahler in a yellowing essay – that his music bristled against symbolization or even choreographic representation; the *Third Symphony* and *Das Lied von der Erde* are quite simply impossible to imagine as ballet music. The author had no idea how soon the unimaginable would become harsh reality. Mahler has been danced, filmed, recorded as a musical treat so that even the pictures on the covers suggest *Swan Lake* or the *Alpen Symphony* – all of this can hardly be acceptable for a reasonable reception of his works.

Karl Kraus, alluding to a well-known remark by Mahler, once said: "I am a mega-lomaniac. I know that my time will not come." Perhaps it will one day turn out that even Mahler could have reason to be a megalomaniac.

Gustav Mahler was buried in the Grinzing Cemetery in Vienna. His tombstone was designed by Josef Hoffmann.

dass i ch ver

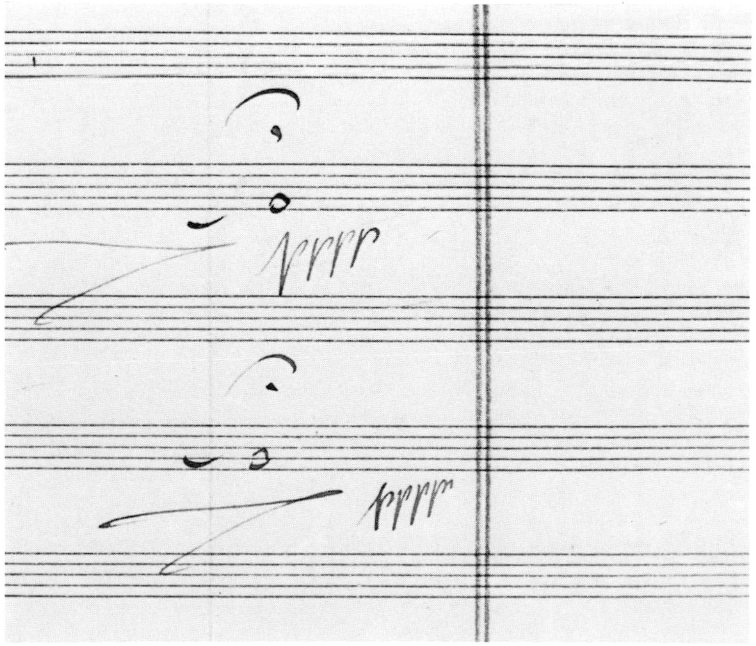

ACKNOWLEDGMENTS

The pictures in this book were taken by Jaroslav Krejci and Jaroslav Svoboda.
Archiv der Wiener Philharmoniker 118, 120, 122/123, 127; Bruno Ballestrini (Electa, Milan) 111; Bildarchiv Preussischer Kulturbesitz (Berlin) 39, 105, 114; Dr. Friedrich C. Heller 121, 141; Historisches Museum (Vienna) 32, 34, 35, 36, 41, 46, 48, 73, 78, 103; A. Huber (Munich) 105 (r); Jaroslav Krejci (Prague) 8/9, 33, 41, 45, 49, 51, 56, 57, 60/61, 77, 78/79, 83, 87, 119, 159/160; Österreichische Nationalbibliothek (Vienna) Archive 4, 5, 10, 11, 16, 17, 18, 19, 20, 21, 23, 24, 27, 29, 30, 31, 38, 39, 43, 50, 52, 53, 54, 55, 58, 62, 65, 67, 68, 69, 71, 73, 74, 75, 85, 86, 88, 89, 90, 91, 92, 101, 103, 104, 105, 106, 109, 112, 113, 115, 117, 129, 131, 141, 143, 144, 146, 147, 151, 152, 155, 157, 161, 162; Österreichische Nationalbibliothek (Vienna) Music Collection 15, 63, 70, 75, 130, 136, 137, 138/139, 158, 163, 165; Österreichische Haus-, Hof- und Staatsarchiv (Vienna) 76, 80, 81; Dr. Dietrich A. Roller (Vienna) 42, 44, 82, 93, 94, 95, 96, 97, 98/99, 100, 134, 135; Thomas-Mann-Archiv (Zürich) 142; Ullstein Bilderdienst (Berlin) 114; Universal Edition (Vienna) 7, 12, 13, 25, 66, 107, 128, 145, 153; Wiener Stadtbibliothek (Vienna) 47, 59, 84, 110, 125, 133, 154, 156; Sigrid Wiesmann (Vienna) 124, 148

The quotations in this book were taken from:
Aaron Copland – "The New Music", New York (4); Arnold Schönberg – The Prague Address, 1913 (6); Gustav Mahler – "Gustav Mahler" by Alma Mahler, London (22); Arnold Schönberg – Letter to Gustav Mahler on 12.12.1904 (26); Richard Strauss – On the occasion of Gustav Mahler's fiftieth birthday, 1910 (28); Bruno Walter – "Gustav Mahler", London, 1958 (30); Gustav Mahler "Gustav Mahler" edited by Willi Reich, Zurich, 1958 (140).

Published in the United States of America
in 1976 by Rizzoli International Publications, Inc. 712 Fifth Avenue, New York 10019
© 1976 by Chr. Belser AG für Verlagsgeschäfte & Co. KG, Stuttgart und Zürich.
First published in German under the title of "Gustav Mahler und Wien".
Library of Congress Catalog Card Number: 76–11243
ISBN: 0–8478–0039–3
Printed in the Federal Republic of Germany by Belser Stuttgart.

CONTENTS